A Sip in Time

India's Finest Teas and Teatime Treats

A Sip in Time

India's Finest Teas and Teatime Treats

PALLAVI NIGAM SAHAY

hachette INDIA

First published in 2022 by Hachette India
(Registered name: Hachette Book Publishing India Pvt. Ltd)
An Hachette UK company
www.hachetteindia.com

1

Photographs by Shabin E. and Yasmin Al-Shaqsi

Cover and book design by Meena Rajasekaran

The views and opinions expressed in this book, and the recipes provided in it, are the author's own and the facts are as reported by her. The publishers are not in any way liable for the same. It is the sole responsibility of any cookbook user to check the list of ingredients, and cooking media provided to determine if any medical condition may arise from the consumption of the ingredients or in any combination of the ingredients in preparation of the recipe. Likewise, all instructions and timelines are for guidance only; and must be correlated to the actual kitchen in use, and utensils or appliances being used for preparation. Readers are advised to exercise a very high level of caution when following a recipe involving any potentially hazardous activity, including the use of high temperatures, open flames and when deep frying. In particular, when frying, add ingredients carefully to avoid splashing, and never leave the pan or flame unattended. The author and the publishers are not responsible for any problems or hazards including but not limited to allergic reactions, accidents or any harm caused during the preparation of any of the recipes in the book.

ISBN 978-93-91028-86-2

Hachette Book Publishing India Pvt. Ltd
4th & 5th Floors, Corporate Centre,
Plot No. 94, Sector 44, Gurugram 122003, India

Printed and bound in India
by Manipal Technologies Limited, Manipal

Athato ghumakkar jigyasa
Mann milla toh mela nahi toh sabse bhala akela

Now for a study of *ghumakkar*, the unquenchable curiosity to wander...
Where minds meet it's a festival, else much better to be alone.

– Mahapandit Shri Rahul Sankrityayan,
Ghumakkar Shastra

For Ma–Papa, Mummy–Papa, Sushmita, Kunal, and every tea lover in the world.

I want to extend my sincere thanks to Parag Hatibarua, Madhurjya Gogoi, Sandeep Gogoi, Pabitra Ningda, Jaulet Manje, Manoj and Leena, Nalanda and Oshi, Boke, Kadu, Pabo, Mahesh Lama, Hrishikesh Lama, Bertie, Rajah Banerjee, Sanjay Das, Sanaya Khan, Sanjith Raju, Yezdi Mistry, Dr Sibby Matthew, Raj Ettan and Chechi, Shabin E., Meena Rajasekaran, Poulomi Chatterjee and the team at Hachette India, and so many others who have helped, guided and blessed me on this beautiful sojourn.

Contents

Introduction

On a cold winter morning in October 2018, I stood on the bank of the River Brahmaputra in Guwahati, and was overcome by the same sense of curiosity that I had felt while exploring the food of Italy during a culinary course there. For someone who is as passionate about tea as I am, the solitude of tea estates feels like a carefully preserved slice of history; the tough, steep terrains of tea tree covered mountains narrates the story of the stubborn human spirit, the dense air seems to resonate with cheerful songs and giggles of those beautiful people who, for generations, have devoted their love and care to these pointy little leaves. A sense of excitement coursed through me, and I was sure that I was about to embark upon a beautiful journey in my tea trails across India.

This story begins with my discovery of black tea in 2011, in that serendipitous moment when I sipped it for the first time. It was the morning after my wedding, and as I joined my parents-in-law for breakfast, they asked what I would like to drink. Feeling a bit shy around my new family, I replied, 'I will have whatever you are drinking.' They were sipping on some Darjeeling first flush and for me, it was love at first sip. From the refreshing, crisp aroma which hit my nose as soon as my mother-in-law poured me a cup to the peachy floral flavours that suffused my senses as I took my first sip and ate the sweet biscuits that complemented its flavours, I was a convert.

Until this point, I had always been a masala chai girl. The typically Indian brew had energized me, calmed me, helped me rejoice in daily triumphs and celebrated my most special moments till I stayed with my parents. Growing up, in the company of both family and friends, we laughed, we gossiped, and we argued around countless cups of chai. In my marital home, this place is occupied by Darjeeling tea. Hardly an hour goes by without my parents-in-law reaching for a cup of this delicate tea. 'It will take time to brew, Pallavi,' Papa, my father-in-law, tells me each time I prepare him a cup of tea. And over the years, whether I am making tea and or am between things, waiting for good news or positive results, that sentiment echoes in my mind and strengthens my faith in the fact that the longer things take to brew, the better their flavours – just like a cup of Darjeeling tea.

Today's world, driven by information technology and social media, keeps us immensely busy, demanding all of our time and attention. In this scenario, tea has become a powerful word as it does not simply manifest a beverage – rather, it manifests a state of calm and peace. With each sip, we find ourselves closer to the deep meditative rhythms of nature in which the tea leaves were born. With every sip that we enjoy in the present, we partake of the past, of those moments when the leaves were plucked, and it is this rejuvenating flavour that deepens our connection with nature in an increasingly virtual world. I believe that it is this sense of being one with nature which makes us fall in love with tea even more deeply.

Over the years, my love for tea has grown to consuming a minimum of seven cups a day. My day starts on the strong, uplifting note of Assam tea and by afternoon, I find myself reaching out for the gentle comfort of Darjeeling tea. By evening, and especially the late evening and night, I want to lose myself in the soothing embrace of a Munnar white or rose tea.

Ma and Papa (my parents-in-law) love sweet snacks like biscuits or cookies with their tea, and I love baking. But since my husband Kunal loves everything chocolate, I mostly baked with chocolate. I found that it never paired well with tea. Now, after years of cooking and baking with chocolate, I have come to understand that it is in the inherent nature of chocolate to overpower every other flavour. But at that point, disappointed with chocolate and at the risk of disappointing Kunal, for once, I pursued a personal pleasure and baked a soft, crumbly, lemon cake one evening, and it synchronized beautifully with the delicate flavours of tea. Since then, I started to understand and respect tea's affinity for unpretentiously sweet, creamy food. It soon became a hobby to plan a menu to go with tea for guests, and there were many hits and a few misses as well. While a successful pairing made me feel confident, a failed one left me curious about the secrets flavours each tea was still hiding. And knowing that tea was cultivated and processed just few states east from where I was, I wanted to visit those towns and taste tea on its native ground.

After publishing my first book, *The Bhojpuri Kitchen*, and finishing filming a food series with Zee Television in the second half of 2018, I suddenly found myself relatively unoccupied. And so, I took the opportunity to pursue the flavours which had been brewing at the back of my mind for so long, and my passion for this beautiful subject began to transform into a lifelong relationship as I joined a tea sommelier course in Guwahati.

My tea sommelier course, or the first phase of my tea trails, answered a lot of my questions such as the difference between CTC, or 'crush, tear and curl' (the granules with which my mother prepares her chai) and wiry, twisted full-leaf tea (which my mother-in-law uses to brew her black tea). I understood why black tea made from Assam has a malty, robust taste which is entirely different from the fruity-floral black tea made from Darjeeling leaves. I delved into the history of the tea leaf to see whether tea was brought to India by the British from China or had it already been growing here? I learned why sweet chai is paired best with salty snacks

(L–R) My mother-in-law, my husband and my father-in-law.

and black tea is fond of sublime sweet snacks. But most importantly, the course introduced me to the great heritage of Indian artisanal teas that have been handcrafted for centuries by the ethnic communities in the pristine environs of the north-east of India.

The more I learnt, the more curious I became, which led me to the second phase of my quest – a journey across the tea towns of India. Like a pilgrim, I travelled the length and breadth of this vast country trying to understand the art and science of the process of making tea. Along the way, I was overwhelmed by the love and affection of the people I met. We connected deeply and soon found a lot of commonalities between us because as a passionate cook and a trained chef, I am accustomed to the seasonality of food just like tea makers and tasters. Meeting people from these communities and witnessing them handcraft teas was the most interesting part of my journey.

This book is a collection of stories, anecdotes and recipes that I gathered during my tea travels, and it starts with a brief account of the types of teas in India and how they are processed. It then proceeds to a narration of tea's ancient existence in India and the traditions of artisanal handcrafted teas. From there, we go to Assam to listen to the story of the strong Assamese black tea becoming a household name in India and the role played by the British in this phenomenon. Then, we find out about the birth of Darjeeling tea, the shining jewel in India's tea crown. After a luxurious tour of the manicured tea estates of Darjeeling, we enter the rugged trails of the tea forests of Arunachal Pradesh and the unique traditional handcrafting methods of its ethnic minorities.

After experiencing the thrills of the hills of the north-east, our tea trail leads us to god's own country, Kerala, to experience not only the unique flavours of Munnar tea but also the uniqueness of their management style. Each chapter is a narration of my own journey, and I have tried to share with you everything through the lens of tea. Along with my adventures, you will also find recipes for my favourite snacks complimenting the flavour profiles of the tea in each chapter.

This book holds a special place in my heart as it chronicles the privilege and satisfaction of meeting people and places that would have otherwise remained unknown to me. My journey through the research, though far from being over, has been fabulously fascinating. Every day would lead to newer discoveries, unfolding sometimes the great adventures of fellow tea travellers, and sometimes acquainting me with centuries-old traditional practices. Drinking tea is happiness as it has both pleasure and purpose. It helps me enjoy the other most intrinsic qualities known to human existence: ease, comfort and space. I hope you find the same in your teacup every day.

From Earth to Palate

As I packed my bags to leave for my tea sommelier course in Guwahati, I could not stop wondering whether tea would taste different on its native ground than it had at home. Would it be purer, more itself somehow? And as I zipped up my bag that night, I realized that for the first time in seven years, I was not carrying pouches of my most trusted companion, Earl Grey. I was hopeful that this sojourn to the earth where my beloved teas were grown would be filled with teas of a superior quality, with teas that I had not tasted before – and I was not wrong.

I was excited to be in Guwahati and explore its food scene, and I knew it would be difficult to wait till the end of the course. So, I had reached Guwahati two days before my course was to start. During those two days, I visited the Kamakhya Temple, wandered through flea markets around the Brahmaputra, saw new varieties of fish and vegetables. I ate super spicy food from Nagaland at the Michinga Restaurant and authentic Assamese food at Paradise Restaurant, which also became my regular eating joints for the rest of my stay. During this time, I also figured out the route for my morning walk. I would walk around Digholi Pukuri, a beautiful pond, which was five minutes from where I stayed. I also had a preliminary meeting with my teacher for the sommelier course, Parag Hathibarua, whom we called Parag Sir. He has spent 32 years in the tea industry as a tea taster and is also the director of the International Tea Masters Association (ITMA).

The course started with an introductory session on the tea plant. There are two main varieties of tea plants, one that is native to Assam and is called *Camellia sinensis var. Assamica*, and the other that is native to China and is referred to as *Camellia sinensis var. sinensis*. There is one more variety of tea plant known as *Camellia sinensis var. Cambodia*, but that is only planted in Cambodia. The Assam variety is a hardy plant and is the most widely planted tea plant in the world, and its Chinese cousin stands next.

In the sessions that followed, we made multiple trips to a tea estate nearby called Sonapur Tea Estate to understand the terroir, or the environmental attributes affecting the tea leaves: temperature, humidity, slope, soil and rains. A unique equilibrium between all these factors results in the healthy growth of the tea plant. Nature has bestowed this bounty to a few special regions south of the Himalayan mountains, including north-eastern India, south-western China, Cambodia, Vietnam and Myanmar, and ancient tea trees have been found here. Some of the plants I saw on my visits to India's tea heartland were centuries old and more than 10 to 15 feet tall whereas the tea bushes in the estates are no taller than 4 feet on average. It is impossible to replicate this unique convergence of climatic conditions anywhere else and that's what makes this tea so special.

For the Assamica variety to flourish, it needs plenty of rainfall, abundant humidity, and not too high or not too low, tropical temperatures. That's why it thrives in the low-lying areas of Assam. On the other hand, the China variety needs much less sun, not more than four or five hours a day, the cool temperatures of the hills, abundant rainfall and mountain mist. It was imported from China, and it could not survive in the heat of Assam, but when it was planted in Darjeeling, it thrived.

Good soil for tea plants is made up of equal proportions of sand and clay. According to Parag, 'the soil should have enough clay to be able to retain water for a continuous supply to the plant, and it should also have sand in equal proportions to prevent swampiness.'

After a few sessions, once we'd gained proper insight into the climatic factors affecting tea, we started our tea tasting sessions. As we entered the tasting room, we saw a collection of white cups and a kettle arranged in a row on a table inside. Each kettle bore the name of the tea inside it. We then poured the tea in the cups and sipped. That day, we tasted Assam, Darjeeling, white, oolong, green, yellow, Pu-erh and purple tea.

'You must suck in as much oxygen as possible while tasting the tea,' said Parag as he made a loud, smacking noise with every sip of tea he tasted, making sure that I did the same. And I could taste the difference – I felt that the flavours were more pronounced than while taking quiet sips. 'The difference in the oxygen level is what makes tea taste different on a flight than on the ground,' he added.

Now, you obviously cannot make such a noise every time you sip tea at home, so the trick to retain oxygen in your tea is not to overboil your water, but just let it come to a gentle simmer and then pour it in your kettle or over the tea bag in your cup and allow it to brew.

Each sip of tea carries caffeine, sweetness and acidity. The difference in the level of these properties defines the flavour of black, white, green, yellow or Pu-erh teas. These differences occur during the processing of the tea leaves, and the method of processing selected depends on the type of leaf. The Assam tea plant is more like a bonsai tree and produces big, broad leaves, which are perfect for processing into strong black tea with a woody and malty flavour. The pointy, little leaves of China bush have a delicate flavour profile and are perfect

for processing into speciality teas such as orthodox black, white, green, oolong, yellow and purple teas.

There are four steps in the processing of tea leaves: withering, rolling, oxidization and drying. The time and duration of these steps is the deciding factor in the type of tea that will be produced.

The first step is withering. After being picked, the leaves are left out to wither, and this starts with spreading them in large wooden troughs with a base made of fine wire mesh, through which warm, gentle air is applied for a minimum of 12 hours. This takes away the excess moisture and makes the leaves crisp enough for the next step, which is rolling.

Rolling is a process in which tea leaves are gently bruised in order to make their juices come out, and these juices will then react to the oxygen in the air and develop caffeine. Centuries ago, the hill tribes of north-east India made tea by rolling tea leaves in between their palms, but to meet the current global demand of tea, this is now done by machines in tea-processing factories. To produce black tea, which holds the largest share in terms of production among India's teas, machine rolling is classified into two categories, orthodox and CTC. In the orthodox method, the ancient hand-rolling method is imitated by machines, and as a result, the tea leaves are gently bruised and left whole. The orthodox method is used to produce tea with milder levels of caffeine. The CTC method is applied to bring out the natural juices of tea leaves and produce strongly caffeinated tea, and we will discuss this method in greater detail later in the book. All of the tea from Darjeeling is processed using the orthodox method, whereas Assam devotes most of its leaves to producing CTC and a very small portion is used to produce orthodox. The process of making white tea doesn't involve any rolling, and green, oolong, yellow and purple teas are given a very gentle orthodox roll. The next step in the process is oxidization.

Oxidization is where all the magic happens. The extent to which the tea leaves have been allowed to oxidize, or develop caffeine, determines the category to which the tea will belong. When the juices on the surface of the leaves have been allowed to stay in the open air long enough to turn the leaf completely red, it is known as full oxidization, and this results in a strongly caffeinated black tea. When the pores on the tea leaf are sealed right before they are about to turn fully red, it is called semi-oxidization and results in a mildly caffeinated oolong tea. When the pores are sealed right after rolling, without allowing the juices at any time to react with oxygen, it is known as unoxidized tea and results in decaffeinated green tea. White tea is a different ball game altogether because this is what you get when the most tender tea leaves are just plucked, withered and dried in the sun. They go through minimum processing which implies no rolling, hence there is no oxidization.

As soon as the tea leaves attain the desired level of caffeine, they are placed on a conveyor belt and passed through a moderate oven, and this step is known as drying. It inactivates the process of oxidization and seals in the flavour. Drying also imparts the beautiful, dark chocolate brown colour to the leaves. After being dried, the leaves are sorted and auctioned. Wholesalers buy, package and sell these leaves to retailers, and this is how our morning cup of chai finds its way to us from the hills of the north-east.

Drinking freshly brewed Phalap with (L–R) tea maker Pabitra Ningda, tea blogger Sandeep Gogoi, tea maker Madhurjya Gogoi. We called it our Phalap tea party.

Pabitra Da sautéing tea leaves in a wok with the help of chopsticks. Wok-firing the tea leaves is the first step involved in making Phalap.

Phalap, India's First Brew

We left Duliajan, a small town in the Dibrugarh district, at dawn, heading north towards Margherita town. An hour into our journey, we stopped for breakfast at a roadside dhaba and were served black tea, a large bowl of spicy chicken curry and rice. My eyes and nose watered as I ate, but I relished every bite. Then, we got back into the car and concrete roads turned into dirt tracks as we continued our journey into the densely forested areas of upper Assam.

I had made the journey to such a remote area being drawn to the legend surrounding Phalap, a variety of black tea handcrafted by the Singphos, a tribe that has dwelled in this region for many centuries. I first found out about the Singphos and their artisanal tea in a class on the indigenous teas of India during my sommelier course. While discussing the origins of tea in India, Parag gave us a full account of the tribe and their methods of handcrafting tea. We will get into those details later in the chapter, but first let me tell you about Phalap's mysterious appearance and playful taste and aroma.

As he was talking about this ancient tea, Parag took a 12-inch-long bamboo stalk from his huge collection of teas and said, 'This is Phalap.' I stared at the bamboo stalk, trying to figure out where the tea was. Then, using his pocketknife, he chopped off one end of the bamboo and slid out a compressed, cylindrical cake of tea leaves. With the same knife, he chopped off a small portion of the cake. Before brewing the Phalap, he gave it to me to look at. When I took a whiff of it, I found that it smelled like a piece of wood which had been slowly burning on charcoal for a long while. And it tasted similar too – like it had been left uncovered near charcoal to absorb those beautiful, smoky notes. I use that technique, known as dhungaar, to smoke my biryanis and kebabs, and it is one of my absolute favourite flavours. Needless to say, I enjoyed Phalap very much. After the tasting, we discussed the method of its making and its history as the first tea in India, which made me curious about the Singphos and I wanted to experience everything for myself.

By mid-morning, we had reached Margherita, and straightaway we went to meet Pabitra Ningda, a Phalap maker, whose family has been handcrafting Phalap for many generations. As we arrived at his home, he greeted us with a hot cup of Phalap and some jaggery (gur) as a snack to be eaten with it. 'This is the traditional way of greeting guests in the Singpho community,' said my companion Madhurjya Gogoi, a friend of Parag who had set out with me from Duliajan. He is a second-generation tea planter and seller, and runs his own tea processing plant in Duliajan. Currently, his overriding obsession is to make premium green tea at an affordable price.

As we sat there, sipping Phalap on its native ground with its maker, I realized that the experience was no less exciting than my experience with parmesan cheese in the Parma region of Italy. The tea and jaggery comforted us with its warmth in the freezing temperatures of the town of Margherita as did Pabitra Da's stories. He shared fond memories of his father and grandfather going deep into the jungle riding on an elephant's back to pluck tea leaves from tea trees that were at least a hundred years old. He showed us tea leaves from his own tea garden, and once we'd finished our tea, he invited us into his kitchen to show us how Phalap was made.

Along with being a skilful Phalap maker, Pabitra Da was a cheerful storyteller, his hand gestured and spoke faster than his mouth. As soon as he'd lit a fire in his earthen stove (juihal), he placed a wok (kadhai) over the fire, added some tea leaves and started to sauté them, all the while stirring with chopsticks. And then, he began to narrate another story. Almost two hundred years ago, he said, his hands flying, there were two Singpho brothers engaged in *jhoom kheti*, or slash-and-burn agriculture. One day, they were both thirsty, and one brother plucked the leaves of a nearby tree. After chewing them, he felt relieved and fresh, and the other brother asked him in the Singpho language, 'Pha lap (what leaf)?' That is how Phalap got its name.

He had taken a moment to point out that this method of roasting the leaves in a wok on top of juihal is called wok firing. As his story came to an end, so did the sautéing, the leaves had by now acquired a copper red hue, indicating that the caffeine had started to develop.

According to Pabitra Da, wok firing was the method of withering followed by the Singphos. This process relieves the tea leaves of their excess moisture and helps develop the distinctly nutty notes. After wok firing, the second step is to dry the leaves in the sun for a day before sealing them in a hollow bamboo shaft. But since we had only a day in Margherita, Pabitra Da used leaves that he had already dried in the sun to show us the process.

For the final step, Pabitra Da took a hollow bamboo shaft, placed it in the mild heat at the centre of the juihal and started swirling it with his hands. This was supposed to help reduce the moisture in the bamboo, ensuring a longer shelf life for the dried tea. After six to seven minutes of roasting, he lifted the bamboo out and started to fill it with the sun-dried tea leaves. He pressed them tightly into the bamboo with the help of a thick, wooden stick. He then peeled off the outer tough skin of the bamboo with a traditional knife known as the dhow, and the green of the bamboo was gone and the white had started to show. Next, he closed the mouth of the bamboo by twisting the edges that had been made pliable by peeling, and he placed it on a wooden platform hanging over the earthen stove. 'We now have to let it sleep peacefully for a minimum of six months. Over time, it will absorb the smoke from the juihal and will develop a distinct smoky note in its flavour and in its aroma. The heat from the stove will ensure a dry environment for our tea leaves,' said Pabitra Da. He also mentioned that aging ensures a mellower, well rounded and earthier flavour in the Phalap leaves.

The next story he narrated was about pruning, a process followed by tea estates in which tea bushes are trimmed to maintain their height till waist level. Pruning helps tea bushes achieve good growth and makes plucking convenient. According to Pabitra Da, it was the Singpho community that invented this process. 'After discovering indigenous tea plants growing wild in the Singpho area, the British government leased the land from the Singphos to grow tea commercially. However, it was not an easy task due to the dense forest, wild animals and lack of resources for commercial production, and as a result, it wasn't profitable. One time, the British government refused to pay the rent on the leased land, and this angered the Singphos. They decided to teach the British a lesson and one night, a few people from the community went to the tea fields and cut the trees to a quarter of their size. But to everyone's surprise, the tea bushes started producing a much better yield! And thus, pruning was invented.'

The day was coming to an end, and so was the time with my new friend Pabitra Da as we had to reach Duliajan before it got too dark. On our way, we stopped at a hotel called the Singpho Eco Lodge for some food and I was pleasantly surprised to see that it was full of tourists. After talking to one of them, I found out that they were from Korea and had come there for the same reason as me – following the wake of Phalap.

I also noticed that the gardens of the Singpho Eco Lodge were full of tea plants, and being curious I spoke to the manager, Jaulet Manje, about whether they made Phalap as well. Jaulet also happened to be the son of the owner of the lodge and gave me a tour of the kitchen where Phalap was being crafted. He showed me piles of Phalap stacked on top of two large earthen stoves; he also told me that his family was currently in Canada where they were participating in a tea expo, a sure sign that the Singphos had successfully managed to put themselves on the world map for their wonderful artisanal tea. It seemed clear to me that as the world moves more and more towards personal ways, towards organic and handcrafted things, the Singphos, or anyone who has managed to stay true to themselves, have a promising future.

Recipes

Meeting people from ethnic communities living a traditional lifestyle can have a long-lasting impression on a visitor. Their sheer simplicity and minimalism are two things that impress you the most. My trip to Margherita on the Phalap trail will always remain remarkably close to my heart because along with discovering new flavours, I also made new friends who were wonderful and open-hearted. Now, whenever I wish to reminisce about those days, all I do is brew a hot cup of Phalap and prepare my favourite jaggery snacks to go with it just the way the Singphos drink it.

Gur ke Parathe (Parathas Stuffed with Jaggery and Coconut)

If you can imagine the caramelly sweetness of jaggery imbued with the nutty flavours of coconut, the earthiness of sesame encased in a salted pastry and seared in ghee, you will understand the flavours of my favourite jaggery snack, gur ke parathe. They are a source of constant delight at my breakfast table, especially on a cold winter day. The gleaming, golden tint of these parathas not only visually compliments the orange-ish hue of Phalap, but also harmonizes well with the tea's sublime, earthy flavours.

An important thing to note – please eat the parathas when they are still warm as jaggery tends to harden once the food becomes cold. Although, there's always the option of reheating afterwards. I recommend using sugarcane jaggery for this recipe as it breaks easily, and I find breaking the jaggery in a pestle and mortar a lot more convenient than grating it. Also, don't replace ghee with oil or any other low fat supplements as it makes a huge difference to the taste.

Prep time: 20 minutes | Cooking time: 15 minutes | Makes: 4

Ingredients

1 cup wholewheat flour
¼ cup water
½ cup sugarcane jaggery
3–4 tbsp grated coconut
3–4 tbsp ghee
A pinch of edible camphor (optional)
Extra flour, for rolling and dusting

Method

1. Add the wholewheat flour to a mixing bowl and slowly pour the water to knead a medium consistency dough. Once the dough is smooth, cover it with a cloth and let it rest it for 15 minutes. This allows the gluten in the flour to rest and the parathas are softer.

2. Meanwhile, break the jaggery in a pestle and mortar. If you don't have one, you can use your rolling pin. Add the jaggery to a medium-sized bowl, add the coconut, 1 tablespoon of ghee and the camphor (if using) and mix well. Set aside.

3. After the dough has rested, pinch out a portion the size of a lime and roll it between your palms to make a smooth ball. Now, place the ball on your work surface, and use your fingers to press it down and

flatten it. Then use a rolling pin to roll it out into a disc of diameter 6 cm.

4. Place a heaped tablespoon of the jaggery mixture in the centre of the disc. Using the back of a spoon, flatten the mixture into a thin, round layer. Then, bring the edges together to close. If required, sprinkle some flour on your rolling surface and use a rolling pin to roll out the disc a bit more. This is the paratha ready to be cooked.

5. Heat a shallow pan, add 1 teaspoon of ghee and spread it. Place the paratha on the pan and cook for 3–4 minutes. After two minutes, lift the paratha with a spatula, add 1 teaspoon of ghee to the pan and put the paratha back on its other side. Again, allow it to cook for 3–4 minutes or until golden brown.

6. Put it on a plate and enjoy your warm, sweet parathas with a hot cup of Phalap.

Thekua

Incredibly crumbly mouthfeel, full of the elegant flavours of cardamom and punctuated with refreshing fennel seeds – this is what Thekua is. A golden nugget of goodness induced with caramelly nuttiness of jaggery and a seared on soft crunch. It is an essential snack for almost all the festivals in Bihar (my marital home). But since its subtle sweetness and soft crispness pair very well with a cup of strong, black tea, my snack jars are often filled with it. To tell you the truth, as much as I love cooking I love the idea of waking up to something fulfilling without having to go inside the kitchen early in the morning, and thekua hits the right spot.

They are not made very flaky in my marital home – actually the flakiness of a thekua differs from home to home, depending upon how generous the cook is feeling while adding shortening (maun). I love the way Ma (my mother-in-law) makes them, and this is her recipe.

The appearance of the thekua has nothing to do with its taste, and it doesn't matter if you don't have a thekua mould. However, you can use a fork to make impressions in any design that you like.

People often add dry fruits to thekua, but those dry fruits mostly surface on top and get burnt while frying. It brings in an unpleasant bitterness which I don't like, and that's why I never add it and recommend not to.

Prep time: 20 minutes | Cooking time: 20 minutes | Makes: 10–15

Ingredients

1 cup water
250 gm jaggery, broken into small pieces
400 gm wholewheat flour

Method

1. Add water and jaggery in a saucepan and bring it to a boil. Keep stirring until the jaggery is totally dissolved. We are not making jaggery syrup, just dissolving jaggery. The moment the jaggery disappears into the water, remove it from the heat and set aside.

150 gm coconut, grated
7–8 green cardamom, coarsely ground
2 tsp fennel seeds
4 tbsp ghee
Oil, for deep frying

2. In a big, deep plate or in a large mixing bowl, add flour, coconut, cardamom powder, fennel seeds and ghee, and using a spatula, mix well. Knead into a stiff dough by gradually pouring jaggery water.

3. Divide into small balls the size of a golf ball and then flatten them. If you are using a thekua mould, flatten the dough on top of the mould and press it gently so that it takes on the impression of the mould. If you are not using a mould, flatten it with your hands and use a fork to make impressions on the thekua.

4. Heat oil in a wok, slide the thekua into the oil, and fry on a low flame till golden brown. Flip it once or twice using the perforated spatula (jhara).

5. Once golden on both sides, take the thekua out on a plate and allow them to cool down before eating.

Alternate method: Bake the thekuas

1. Preheat the oven to 180 degrees Celsius.

2. Arrange the raw thekuas on a baking tray and brush a little bit of oil, preferably sunflower oil, on both sides. Bake for around 15–20 minutes or till they are brown. Keep checking if they are done in between.

Instant Makhana Candy (Instant Fox Nut Candy)

This is one of my favourite recipes for when I need that instant pick me up which – let's face it – can only be provided by sugar. And jaggery is a much safer route.

If you like the flavours of caramel popcorn, you will love these fox nut candies (makhana candies).

Makhanas are celebrated all over our country for their rich calcium content, and this recipe not only enhances their health quotient but also makes them irresistible. Think of white makhanas crisped up in desi ghee and wrapped in a shiny sheen of deep amber coloured nutty caramel, they are simply divine.

Allow them to cool a bit before eating, but don't let them go cold in the pan as the jaggery will harden and stick to the pan. In case this happens, reheat the pan gently to release the caramel. In case you are planning to eat it in some time, take the makhanas out on a serving plate and let them rest there. The crunch of the fox nuts will only increase while resting on the plate, which I adore and do on purpose sometimes.

Prep time: None! | Cooking time: 5 minutes | Serves: 2

Ingredients

½ tbsp ghee
1 cup makhana
2 tbsp jaggery, broken into small pieces
A pinch of salt

Method

1. Heat a shallow pan with ghee and then add the makhanas. Roast them on a low flame for 3–4 minutes, stirring once or twice.
2. Sprinkle the jaggery and salt and stir gently till jaggery melts and coats the makhanas.
3. Transfer to a bowl and serve with a cup of Phalap.

Assam and the Story of Masala Chai

Chai has been such a vital element of my existence that it is difficult to pinpoint my first experience of it. As a child, I remember enjoying *kadha*, a concoction made by boiling tea leaves (chai patti) with a few whole spices, milk, sugar and a pinch of salt. According to my mother, enjoying kadha sip by sip was my favourite part of getting sick. I loved that hint of saltiness against the sweetness of sugar and pepperiness of whole spices. It helped me feel so much better.

India's love affair with chai lacks no proof – from fancy cafés to dhabas, from tapris to thelas, you can see the proof of our passion for chai everywhere. Sometimes, I genuinely believe that Indians have chai instead of blood running through their veins! One of the most beautiful examples of how integral chai is to us are train journeys. Most of us have a memory of the irresistible aroma of the strong, cardamom-infused chai that the chaiwallah, who hopped into your bogie as soon as the train stopped at a station, brought in. I remember that he would make his way through the carriages holding an aluminium kettle in one hand and earthen kulhars in the other shouting, 'Chai garam, garam chai (Hot tea)!' Regardless of whether we're talking about the kulhar chai on Indian trains, Mumbai's cutting chai, or Haryana's khadi chammachwaali chai, Himachal Pradesh's Kinnauri chai, Rajasthan's Nagori chai, Pune's Amrutulya chai, Hyderabad's highway chai, enjoyed by truck drivers and called 'Do sau meelwaali chai,' or Kolkata's famous masala chai – they are all made by boiling brown tea granules in water till that lovely reddish-copper colour appears.

These granules, found across the length and breadth of the country, belong to the category of black tea and are technically called CTC, which is both the name of the tea and the method by which they are processed. It is a slightly different, but much more commercially efficient method of producing black tea compared to the orthodox method in which the leaves are left whole. A majority of India wakes up to the bold flavours of CTC, and they are not just granules but power granules. Indeed, our grandmothers' remedies for a mild headache to a bad throat comprise nothing but chai.

The lion's share of India's CTC, or chai patti, comes from Assam, and it is globally famous for the beautiful malty and woody flavours of its CTC. Apart from being so beloved in India, two world renowned blends, Earl Grey and English Breakfast, are also made using CTC from Assam. The main reason for the beautiful rich, rustic flavours in Assamese CTC lies in its humid, lowland climate. 'For a tea bush to thrive, three factors have to be in sync: the soil, the monsoon and the humidity,' says Parag. And Assam is singular in this convergence, blessed as it is with the mighty Bramhaputra River flowing through the middle of the state, making the soil rich and fertile. The huge fence provided by the great Himalayas in the north not only blocks the cold air from the north but also prevents the inland moisture-laden air from dispersing, giving rise to tropical weather conditions, which manifests as a six-month-long monsoon from June till November and produces a huge amount of heat and humidity. As a result, tea bushes thrive in the moisture created by this humidity and grow abundantly.

According to most tea experts, the tea plant, *Camellia sinensis*, is believed to have originated in the areas south of the Himalayas in a region that consists of Assam and the neighbouring Yunnan province of China. Both regions share the favourable climatic conditions required for the growth of the broad-leaved variety of *Camellia sinensis*, which was found growing indigenously in the jungles of Assam and thus named *Camellia sinensis var. Assamica*. The Assam tea plant is more like a bonsai – it has a strong trunk with a ramifying branch system. The leaves from the *Camellia sinensis var. Assamica* are larger and broader in comparison to *Camellia sinensis sinensis*, and this helps produce a strong, robust brew which is more suitable for processing into CTC rather than speciality teas.

On a trip to the Sonapur Tea Factory a few kilometres outside Guwahati, I learnt about the four processes that convert juicy green tea leaves into the miniscule brown particles we know as chai patti. To begin with, the leaves are put through the process of withering, which means drying of extra moisture from the surface of leaves. The second process is where the magic happens for CTC tea. The leaves are crushed, torn and curled inside a big machine that is divided in three parts. The first part of the machine crushes the leaves, the second tears them into tiny pieces, and the third curls them between two rolling cylinders to make them round. This crushing, tearing and curling ruptures the cells on the surface of tea leaves and helps release all their natural juices and turn them into granules.

As part of the third process, also known as oxidization, the CTC leaves are spread out on big sheets for five to six hours in order to make the juices on the surface of the tea leaf granules react with the oxygen in the atmosphere. This will initiate the development of the caffeine in the tea leaves. In five to six hours, this development will be complete, and the granules will turn red and will be ready for the fourth process.

In the fourth process known as drying, the leaves are loaded on a conveyor belt and passed through a fire oven which stops the oxidization, seals in the flavour and gives the leaf their brown colour. From the oven, the conveyor belt continues to a huge cauldron, in which the dried tea granules are collected and then they reach us via auctions, wholesalers and retailers. As I have mentioned in Chapter 2, the Singpho and many other tribes in the north-east of India have been making tea for many centuries now. But the story of tea becoming a household favourite across the country starts with it being discovered by Major Robert Bruce.

According to Sir Percival Griffith's book, *The History of the Indian Tea Industry*, Robert Bruce was a venturesome businessman who went to upper Assam in search of trade. With the East India Company's permission, he became the agent for Purandhar Singh, a local chief whom the Company was backing in the struggle for control of upper Assam. In 1823, Robert Bruce learnt of the existence of tea in Assam and entered an agreement with a Singpho chief to obtain a tea plant and some seeds. But then, as Jeff Koehler mentions in his book *Darjeeling: A History of the World's Greatest Tea*, two events changed the course of things.

In 1824, the first Anglo-Burmese War took place in response to Assam being largely overrun by the invading Burmese. That same year Bruce, by then a major in the Bengal Artillery, died. His story ends abruptly, and the thread gets taken up by his younger brother, Charles Alexander Bruce. The younger Bruce, evidently tipped off by his sibling before he died, got hold of tea samples, which he sent on to the East India Company in Assam, who, in June 1825, forwarded the packet of leaves and seeds to the Company's botanical gardens for verification. However, these were rejected as they did not belong to *Camellia sinensis*.

What made Major Robert Bruce go looking for tea in the wilds of upper Assam was England's obsession with tea. England was introduced to tea in 1662 with the wedding of Charles II and the Portuguese princess, Catherine of Braganza, a tea lover, whose dowry consisted of the islands of Bombay along with chests of tea from China. She started serving the beverage at court, and it soon became popular.

Up to that point, England had been importing all their tea from China, but given China's strict business policies, it was, increasingly, becoming a difficult trade. The Chinese didn't want anything but Spanish silver in exchange for their beloved tea, and this started depleting England's silver reserves. As a result, the British began to look for suitable land to grow tea. In 1833, a committee was formed in India under Lord William Bentinck, the first governor general of British-occupied India, to follow Robert Bruce's lead. Soon they discovered that the local Singpho and Kamptee tribes were processing local teas using traditional, handcrafting methods and drinking it as their staple beverage.

After this discovery, Charles Alexander Bruce was brought into the picture again. He had lived in Assam for many years, which made him highly knowledgeable about tea-growing areas in the state and the processing and crafting methods practised by local tribes. Upon being contacted by the committee, Bruce quickly assembled a workforce and started setting up tea gardens, but conditions were not that easy. Trying to create a tea garden for commercial production was extremely difficult due to the dense forests, dangerous wildlife and unavailability of technical know-how. Bruce worked with a few Chinese nationals, who had been brought there by the committee to support the plantation set-up, but despite all the obstacles, Bruce and his men didn't give up.

By 1837, with the help of his workers and some help from the Singpho community, they were able to send a significant quantity of the tea they had grown to the East India Company's headquarters in Kolkata. NingroLa, a tea artisan from the Singpho community, played a vital role in the cultivation process, and his descendants still cultivate and make artisanal tea in the Tinsukia district of Assam. After conducting a thorough tasting of the tea, the committee declared it to be of good quality. Finally, in May 1838, a dozen boxes of tea, reinforced with strong tin boxes, sailed for England from Kolkata.

On 10 January 1839, the tea from Assam was auctioned in England, and was sold at 34 shillings per box, which was much higher than the regular price of two shillings per box. This quote from Jeff Koehler's book tells us clearly how much the British loved our Assam tea in London, 'The general opinion of the collected tea brokers and dealers with whom the room was crowded, was that the Assam tea is not only valuable as curiosity... but that the tea itself is of very superior quality being of a pleasant flavour and of such strength that some asserted that the fifth water from it was as strong as the first.' Another shipment was sent to London in early 1840, and a second auction took place on 17 March 1840. A new company was formed by the British government in order to make the maximum gains from their golden discovery known as the Assam Company, and that's how commercial tea plantations in India started.

Maniram Dewan, prime minister to the last Ahom king Purandhar Singh, was the first Indian to grow tea commercially in Assam in the mid-1840s in a place known as Cinnamara in Jorhat. He was followed by many other Indian planters and soon, 16 pioneering Assam tea planters formed an association known as Assam Tea Planters Association. The high profitability of the tea industry soon lured the Marwaris, the business class from Rajasthan to explore the industry. They travelled from Rajasthan to find their fortune in tea cultivation, and Navrang Rai, the father of Harbilas Agarwal, the owner of the Deesha Tea group, became the first Marwari to migrate from Churu and settle in Tezpur. A few years later, he was joined by a stream of traders from Rajasthan. From Tezpur, the Marwaris spread to Dibrugarh and then to various parts of Assam. From that point, the tea industry has played a crucial role in the Indian economy. The industry is one of the key employment generators in the country, particularly for women and the under-privileged in lesser developed areas.

In 1901, the Tea Association of India, which had been formed in 1882 to develop the market for Indian tea, started a massive campaign to make the drink popular within the country. Tea stalls were set up in factories, coal mines and cotton mills, and workers were allowed tea breaks. Tea shops were set up in the large towns, cities, and ports, and this is where the journey of tea becoming intrinsic to Indian culture started. Now, we can't imagine a single day without our chai. As much as it helps us enjoy our happy moments, it also sustains us through tough ones. Whether to unwind or to invigorate, for peace or for pleasure, it's always a cup of tea we reach for.

Growing up, I remember being scolded by my grandmother if I ever served a guest a cup of chai without any accompaniments. She believed that serving chai without snacks was an insult to the guest. Well, I always try to follow what I am told by my elders and therefore, dear reader, the following section contains recipes of some of my favourite snacks to enjoy with chai.

Masala Chai

Prep time: None! | Cooking time: 5–6 minutes | Serves: 2

Ingredients

1½ cup water
1 clove
2 green cardamoms
1 small stick of cinnamon
3–4 black peppercorns
1 small piece of ginger, peeled and crushed
A few rose petals (optional)
2 tsp sugar
1 tbsp Assam CTC tea leaves
½ cup milk

Method

1. Add the water to a saucepan on medium heat, add all the whole spices, ginger and rose petals. Let it come to a boil. Reduce the flame and let it come to a boil again. Add the sugar and tea leaves, simmer for 3–4 minutes or until the water is a nice copper colour.

2. Add the milk, increase the heat to full and let it come to a boil. Then, reduce the heat and let it come to a boil again.

3. Strain into cups and serve the hot masala chai with snacks of your choice.

Monsoon

As soon as the sky opens up and the rain starts to pour, nothing can stop my heart from craving something spicy, something crispy, something deep fried. The sizzling of food being deep fried rhymes well with the rhythms of the falling rains – it always makes me feel warm and cocooned inside my home as the world outside is awash with rain. Each recipe in this section is my way of finding warmth and hope when the dark clouds have somehow managed to get themselves in the way of sunlight.

Mirchi Pakoras (Stuffed Chilli Pepper Fritters)

I got through college spending more time in the canteen than in the classroom. One of my fondest memory from those days is of having morning chai with my friend Deepika, discussing everything from people and clothes, food, books to exams and families. We studied different subjects and our classes were separate, but before heading off in different directions, we would plan to meet for a cup of evening tea. In that pursuit, we never forgot to ask the canteen guy what he'd be serving with the evening chai. When the answer was mirchi pakoras, it suddenly became really easy to get through the day. These golden, crunchy pakoras are a recipe from Tamil Nadu – just like the guys who managed the canteen.

I love mirchi pakoras for their refreshing, rugged flavours, especially with a dash of coconut-garlic chutney. Each bite is a beautiful contrast between their crispy, salty exterior and a tangy, tender interior. They are now a regular companion to chai at home as its sweet taste is elevated by their peppery goodness.

Prep time: 20 minutes | Cooking time: 15 minutes | Makes: 10

Ingredients

For the batter

2 cups gram flour (besan)
2/3 cup water
A pinch of salt
1 tsp red chilli powder
10 Bhavnagri chillies
Oil, for deep frying

Method

1. Make the batter first as it needs time to rest. Add the gram flour, salt and red chilli powder to a medium-sized bowl and gradually add water while continuously whisking with a whisk or fork. Form a very thick batter at first, and ensure there are no lumps. Add a bit more water to bring it to medium consistency. Set aside and allow the batter to rest for at least 20 minutes. Resting the batter will remove the graininess of the gram flour.

2. Wash the chillies and dry them with a kitchen towel. Make a slit down the centre to make space for the stuffing. If you don't want the pakoras to be very spicy, remove the seeds. Set chillies aside.

For the stuffing
3 heaped tbsp tamarind (imli) paste
6 heaped tbsp gram flour
½ tsp carom seeds (ajwain)
½ tsp red chilli powder
½ tsp cumin (jeera) powder
Salt, to taste

To serve
Store-bought dry
coconut-garlic chutney

3. To make the stuffing, in a small pan, dry roast the gram flour till it becomes aromatic and is on the verge of changing colour. Add the roasted gram flour to a bowl, add the red chilli powder, cumin powder, carom seeds, tamarind paste and salt. Mix well and taste to adjust seasoning. Hold a chilli open with your hand and stuff it properly. You can try using a spoon, but using your hands is often more convenient and faster.

4. In a deep pan, heat the oil to deep fry the chillies. Once the oil is hot enough, dip the stuffed chillies in the batter, make sure it is properly coated, and fry on high heat till the batter is cooked and crisp. Flip the chillies once or twice using a perforated spatula.

5. Using the same perforated spatula, gently take the pakoras out of the wok and place them on a plate lined with absorbent paper. Allow them to cool for 10 minutes. Chop them into smaller pieces or serve them whole with a cup of masala chai.

Crispy Paneer Nuggets

While I was working at the Grand Hyatt, I spent hours making these nuggets as they were served as the complimentary starter, and they were so good that everyone kept asking for more!

One of the reasons I love these nuggets is because my time at the Grand Hyatt in Mumbai is amongst the most glorious times of my life. Being surrounded by people who shared my love for food always made me feel at home. Now, whenever I roll these crispy paneer nuggets in the quiet of my kitchen, I relive the hustle and bustle and the thrill of being in a professional kitchen.

These beautiful golden morsels are now my go-to option for a menu for a chai party. They are easy to make, and the sweet chai loves their soft, creamy mushiness covered by a golden, crispy coating.

Prep time: 15 minutes | Cooking time: 10 minutes | Makes: 8–10

Ingredients

For the filling

1 tbsp oil
2 cloves of garlic, chopped
2 green chillies, chopped
1 small onion, chopped
1 cup grated paneer
½ cup grated processed cheese
¼ bunch coriander, finely chopped
Juice of ½ lemon
Salt, to taste
½ tsp chaat masala

Method

1. Heat 1 tablespoon of oil in a small pan, add the garlic and sauté for 1 minute. Add the green chilli and the onion. Sauté till the onion is pink and then turn off the heat. Transfer the mixture to a medium-sized bowl and let it cool for five minutes. Add the grated paneer, cheese, chopped coriander, lemon, salt and chaat masala. Mix everything together and taste for salt and seasoning.

2. Place around a heaped tablespoon of the mixture between your palms and roll it into lemon-sized nuggets. Repeat till the mixture is finished.

For the batter
1 cup all-purpose flour (maida)
Salt, to taste
¼ cup water
1 cup cornflakes
Oil, for deep frying

3. Heat enough oil to deep fry in a deep saucepan. While the oil is heating, make the coating for the nuggets.

4. To make the batter, add the flour to a small bowl, add salt and make a batter of coating consistency by gradually pouring water. Place the cornflakes in a plate and crush them with your hands.

5. To fry the nuggets, first dip a nugget in the coating batter, then roll it in the crushed cornflakes, making sure that it is properly coated. Repeat for all the nuggets. Once the oil is hot enough, fry the nuggets in batches of three or four for a couple of minutes.

6. Using a perforated spatula, gently take the nuggets out and place them on a plate lined with absorbent paper. Allow them to rest for 10 minutes before eating.

2.0L

Spicy Macaroni with Garlic and Spinach

When it is drizzling outside and you don't feel like leaving the cosy comfort of your couch or the beautiful view from your window, this is the recipe you need. It takes both minimum ingredients and effort but delivers maximum flavour. The flavours of all four ingredients of the dish – garlic, spinach, chillies and cheese – gel out beautifully into each other like a marriage made in heaven.

I always keep some macaroni in my store cupboard so that I can rustle up a quick meal anytime I need to. You can use any pasta you like, but I would recommend macaroni because they act as tiny pouches that fill up with the creamy, garlicky sauce. When you take a bite, each piece of macaroni bursts in your mouth with a big punch of flavours which I enjoy very much, and I am sure you will too.

I just happened to have spinach in my refrigerator when I was making this dish, and you can replace it with whatever you have on hand: capsicum, mushrooms, broccoli or even cauliflower. All these flavours work very well with garlic, chilli and cheese. You can also use any vegetable oil in place of olive oil.

Prep time: 5 minutes | Cooking time: 10 minutes | Serves: 1

Ingredients

1 cup uncooked macaroni
1 tbsp olive oil
1 big clove of garlic (or 2–3 small ones), chopped
2 cups spinach leaves, washed and chopped

Method

1. To cook the macaroni, heat water in a pan of water. Once it comes to a boil, salt it generously, add the macaroni and let it boil till the pasta is cooked. Reserve ¼ cup of pasta cooking liquid and set it aside. Now, drain the macaroni.

2. To prepare the sauce, in a pan, heat the oil on a medium flame, add the garlic, sauté for few seconds and then add the chilli flakes and spinach. Allow it to cook till the spinach is soft.

2 tsp chilli flakes
½ cup milk
¼ cup or 3–4 heaped tbsp cheese, grated
1 tbsp parmesan cheese (optional)
Salt, to taste
Cheese, to serve

3. Add the reserved pasta water. Add the milk and let it simmer for 3–4 minutes. Then, add the cheese, and allow it to cook for two more minutes.

4. Now, toss in the pasta and salt and mix well. Cook for 2 more minutes till the pasta absorbs all the goodness of the sauce and then take it off the heat.

5. Serve some in your favourite bowl and sprinkle some cheese on top. Enjoy these spicy flavours enhanced by the contrasting sweetness of your masala chai.

Mumbai Masala Sandwich

I spent two years studying at Mumbai University, trying to understand the theories of great economists like Adam Smith, David Ricardo and Amartya Sen, but I am sorry to say that I did not understand a thing. But what I did understand very vividly, though, were the flavours of the butter-seared Mumbai masala sandwich sold at a stall right outside the university. I think I became addicted to it after my first bite – for many days, it became my morning, afternoon and evening meal!

I admit that it is a bit time-consuming to prepare, but I promise that the end result is totally worth it. Cut the sandwich into two while it is still hot and crisp and experience its magic smothered with pudina–hari mirch (mint–green chilli) chutney or ketchup. Coupled with sweet masala chai, it is a very fulfilling experience.

In case you don't have fenugreek (methi powder) in your store cupboard, add ½ tsp of fenugreek seeds along with the cumin seeds jeera at the start of the recipe. But please do not skip it as its brings a balancing earthiness to the flavours and keeps the sandwiches light on the tummy.

Also, you may use brown bread if you like, but half of the taste of this sandwich comes from that nostalgia imbued sweet crispness of rustic white bread, which is very difficult to get with brown bread.

Prep time: 30 minutes | Cooking time: 15 minutes | Makes: 4

Ingredients
1 tbsp refined oil
1 tsp cumin seeds
1-inch piece of ginger, crushed or chopped

Method

1. To make the potato filling, first heat the oil in a medium-sized pan. Add the cumin seeds and let them crackle. Add the ginger, green chillies and garlic, and sauté for 2 minutes. Add the onions, sprinkle some salt and sauté till slightly brown.

1 tsp green chilli, chopped (optional)
3–4 cloves of garlic, crushed or chopped
1 large onion, chopped
Salt, to taste
1 tsp red chilli powder
½ tsp turmeric powder
¼ tsp fenugreek powder
1 tbsp coriander powder
2 boiled potatoes, mashed
1 tsp garam masala powder
½ tsp dry mango powder (amchur)
½ tsp chaat masala
1 tbsp fresh coriander, chopped
8 slices white bread
Butter, as necessary

For the green chutney
2 cups coriander, chopped
1 cup mint leaves, chopped
1 clove of garlic
1–2 green chillies
1 tsp cumin powder
½ tsp black salt
¼ cup tamarind water
1–2 tbsp of water, if required

2. Then, add the red chilli, turmeric, fenugreek and coriander powders, mix well and sauté for 2 minutes. Add the potatoes, garam masala, dry mango and chaat masala powders, chopped coriander and salt, and mix well. Take the pan off the heat and cool for 5–6 minutes.

3. For the chutney, remove the thick stalks of the coriander and mint. Add to a grinder jar along with the rest of the ingredients for the chutney and grind till smooth.

4. To make the sandwich, take two slices of white bread, spread the chutney generously on both slices. Spread a generous amount of potato stuffing on one slice and cover it with another slice.

5. Put a medium-sized pan on the heat, melt ½ tablespoon of butter and sear the sandwich on both sides till crisp.

6. Cut it with a sharp knife, smother it with chutney and enjoy with your tea.

Chicken Kathi Roll

I often invite friends home for chai, and they come over expecting more than just plates full of something to nibble on between chai and conversations. They come with the expectation of some substantial eating, and this is what I offer them: a soft, fluffy paratha wrapped around bites of spicy chicken, doused in tamarind chutney, made crunchy with lemon-soaked slices of pink-purplish onion. Rolls or wraps, I find, are the most convenient ways of feeding people substantially while maintaining the informalities of a chai party because you don't need too many spoons and plates.

I know making the imli chutney sounds like a lot of effort but in truth it is not. All you have to do is soak, sieve and simmer. Another thing that you need to keep in mind – do not skip sprinkling the *kala namak* or black salt. It is essential as it really takes the flavours to the next level. In fact, to ensure an even spread I use a tea strainer while sprinkling it, the same way I sprinkle icing sugar on top of a cake.

To make things easier, you can prepare the stuffing a day before you are planning to eat the rolls because it only gets better with time. The knowledge that the stuffing is ready and resting in the refrigerator makes preparing the parathas a relaxed process – because all that is left to do is to stuff it and roll it.

The inspiration for these divine rolls comes from my favourite café called Bake n' Shake in Bhopal. After having tried them there, I knew that I had to make these at home. And since then, I haven't stopped!

Prep time: 15 minutes | Cooking time: 30 minutes | Makes: 3–4

Ingredients

1 large onion, chopped
Lemon juice
1 cup boneless chicken, cut into bite-sized pieces
2 tbsp + 1 tbsp oil per wrap
2 onions, thinly sliced

Method

1. Put the sliced onion in a bowl, add lemon juice and set aside.

2. If you are unable to find bite-sized boneless chicken at your supermarket, then buy chicken breasts and if possible, request the butcher in the supermarket to cut them into bite-sized pieces. You can also do this at home. Cover your chopping board with cling film or foil before chopping chicken for easier clean up. Cut 1-cm thick strips from the chicken breast and then chop the strips in 1-inch pieces.

½-inch piece of ginger, chopped
3–4 cloves of garlic, smashed or chopped
Black salt, to taste
½ tsp turmeric powder
1 tsp coriander powder
1 tsp red chilli powder
2 tsp garam masala powder
1tbsp water
1 tbsp yogurt
1 heaped tbsp mint, chopped
1 heaped tbsp fresh coriander, chopped
One medium-sized paratha
(See Egg Roll recipe on page 59)
1 egg (for each wrap)
1 heaped tbsp of tamarind chutney
(See Matar ki Kachori recipe on page 63)
1 tbsp fresh coriander, for garnish

3. Heat 2 tablespoons of oil in a pan, add the onion and sauté till brown. Add the ginger and garlic and sauté for 1 minute. Then, add the salt and the turmeric, coriander and red chilli powders, garam masala and 1 tablespoon of water and mix well. Sauté for 2–3 minutes. Add the yogurt and simmer for 2 minutes. Add the chicken, mix well and simmer till it is cooked. Take off the heat, add the mint and coriander leaves, mix well and let it cool a bit.

4. To make the roll, crack an egg in a bowl, season and then whisk it. Heat 1 tablespoon of oil in a pan. Add the whisked eggs, let them cook halfway and place the paratha on top of it. Flip to cook on the other side just for a minute so that the paratha becomes flexible enough to roll. The egg not only adds flavour, but it also forms a layer which protects the roll from becoming soggy after the chicken stuffing is added.

5. Now, place the egg paratha on a plate and using a tea strainer, sprinkle black salt over the roll. Now, place the stuffing in the centre of the roll and generously drizzle with the tamarind chutney. Garnish with slices of lemon-soaked onions and chopped coriander.

6. Roll the paratha firmly and wrap the bottom half of the roll with foil paper.

Aloo Bonda (Spicy Stuffed Potato Fritters)

There is something immensely powerful about aloo bonda – just the name evokes a sensational taste in the mouth and memory – in fact, my list of favourite foods to pair with chai can never be complete without it. I think this is partly a function of nostalgia. When I was a child, these glorious golden clusters and chai were the most common way to celebrate everyday joys like small gatherings, new additions to the family, scoring good marks in exams and India winning a cricket match.

I love aloo bonda and I make them whenever I am in mood for their salty, soft crunchiness with the spicy potato filling inside. It has taken me some time to come to this realization, but now I don't believe in waiting for an excuse to enjoy myself. Instead, I turn any regular occasion into a joyous one by eating what I love and that too with my best friend, chai.

Prep time: 30 minutes | Cooking time: 30 minutes | Makes: 8–10

Ingredients

For the masala paste

½-inch piece of ginger
3–4 cloves of garlic
1 green chilli
1 whole dried red chilli
2–3 black peppercorns
1 black cardamom
2 green cardamoms
1-inch stick of cinnamon
1 tsp coriander seeds
1 tsp cumin seeds

Method

1. Add all the ingredients for the masala paste to a mixer jar, add a bit of water and grind into a smooth paste. Transfer to a bowl and set aside.

2. Next, prepare the batter for the bondas as it needs some time to rest. In a big bowl, add the gram flour and then gradually add water while mixing continuously to form a smooth batter. Add the salt and red chilli powder and mix well. Taste and season according to your preference.

For the batter

½ cup gram flour
⅓ cup water
1 tsp salt
½ tsp red chilli powder
Oil, to fry

For the potato stuffing

3 large potatoes, boiled
1 tbsp refined oil
1 tsp cumin seeds
1 large onion, sliced
½ tsp turmeric powder
½ tsp red chilli powder
1 tsp coriander powder
1 tsp garam masala powder
½ tsp dried mango powder
Salt, to taste

3. To prepare the stuffing, peel the boiled potatoes and mash them. Heat the oil in a pan, add the cumin seeds and allow them to crackle. Add the sliced onions and sauté till golden brown. Then, add the masala paste and sauté till the oil starts to separate or for 3–4 minutes until fragrant. Add turmeric, red chilli and coriander powders, garam masala and sauté for 2 minutes. Add the mashed potato and dried mango powder to the pan and mix well. Taste the mixture and adjust spices if required. Cool the stuffing for a few minutes and shape into medium-sized balls. Set aside.

4. In another pan, heat oil to deep fry the bondas. Dip the potato balls into the batter, coat well and slide into the oil. Fry till golden and drain the extra oil by placing it on an absorbent tissue.

5. Serve hot with your favourite chutney, although I prefer to have mine plain with a cup of sweet tea.

Kolkata Vegetable Chop

As we all know, deep frying makes everything taste good, and this is something that our Bengali bondhus, our friends from Kolkata, discovered a long time ago. A number of snacks available there are deliciously deep fried, and I tasted these vegetable chops at a street shop on Park Street. An old woman sat on a wooden stool and was continuously frying them while her son wrapped them in newspaper packets for the long line of people waiting there.

One bite, and I fell in love with these tiny parcels of flavour. With the crunch of the deep-fried breadcrumb crust and the earthy, fennel-scented stuffing inside, Kolkata's vegetable chops and chai are just meant to be together.

I have Vikas, my friend and the head chef at Kolkata's beloved café Flury's, to thank for this recipe.

Prep time: 40 minutes | Cooking time: 10 minutes | Makes: 15–20

Ingredients

For the spice blend

1 tsp cumin seeds
1 tbsp fennel seeds
1 tsp black peppercorns
1-inch stick of cinnamon
2–3 dried red chilli
3 cloves
4 green cardamoms
2 black cardamoms
½ tsp fenugreek seeds

Method

1. To make the spice blend, toast all the whole spices in a pan. Once they are fragrant, add them to a mixer jar and grind into a fine powder. Set aside until required.

2. Now, in a pan, dry roast the peanuts till black specks start to appear on the skin. Transfer to a bowl and set aside until required.

3. Start making the stuffing by heating oil in a wok, add the ginger paste and green chilli and fry for half a minute. Add the beetroot and a pinch of salt. Mix well and sauté till the beetroot becomes soft. Now, add the carrots and mix well. Add a pinch of salt and sauté till carrots are soft.

For the mixture
2 tbsp peanuts, halved
1 tbsp ginger paste
2–3 green chillies, finely chopped
½ kg beetroot, finely chopped
Salt, to taste
½ kg carrot, finely chopped
½ kg potatoes, boiled and peeled
2 tbsp coconut, chopped
3–4 tbsp all-purpose flour
5–6 tbsp breadcrumbs
2 eggs, whisked
Oil, for deep frying + 4 tbsp for preparing the stuffing

4. Mash the boiled potatoes and add to the wok. Then, add dry spice powders, coconut and peanuts and mix well. Taste and adjust for salt. Let the mixture cool a little and then start making medium-sized cylindrical cutlets.

5. Now, set up your breadcrumbing station. Add flour to a plate, breadcrumbs to another plate and eggs to a bowl. Season everything with salt, mix and whisk thoroughly.

6. Dip the prepared cutlets first in the flour, then in the eggs and finally, roll them in the breadcrumbs. Make sure they are properly coated. Sometimes, I double-coat the cutlets in breadcrumbs, which simply means after they are breadcrumbed once, I dip them in the eggs again and roll them in the breadcrumbs a second time. This helps form a more crunchy crust.

7. In a deep pan, add the oil and place the pan over high heat. It is important that the oil is hot, or the coating will slide into the oil. Add the cutlets and deep fry till beautifully golden brown. They will only need a minute or so on each side. Flip them once using a perforated spatula. As soon as they are golden in colour, take them out and drain the extra oil by placing it on an absorbent tissue.

8. Serve with a hot cup of masala chai.

Beguni (Brinjal Pakoras/Eggplant Fritters)

This is just what I need when the rain is pitter-pattering down my window: the mushiness of brinjal wrapped cosily inside a salty, puffy, golden crunchy coating suffused with the warmth and goodness of carom seeds. And for me, to make the moment feel complete, that divine crispness has to be followed by the sweetness of masala chai.

Prep time: 40 minutes | Cooking time: 10 minutes | Makes: 15–20

Ingredients

1 cup gram flour
½ cup water
2 large brinjals
Salt, to taste
1 tbsp cornflour
1 tsp green chilli, finely chopped
1 tbsp fresh coriander, chopped
½ tsp carom seeds
½ tsp nigella seeds (kalonji)
1 tsp red chilli powder
A pinch of turmeric powder
A pinch of garam masala powder
Chaat masala, to sprinkle
Oil, for deep frying

Method

1. To make the batter, put the gram flour in a medium-sized bowl and gradually add water to form a very thick batter. Once you are sure there are no lumps, you can add more water to bring it to a medium consistency. Set aside and allow the batter to rest for at least 20 minutes.

2. To prepare the brinjals, wash and dry them and slice them to get 1/4-inch thick roundels out of them. Place each slice on a tray, sprinkle a bit of salt and leave for 10 minutes. Then, wipe off the moisture with the help of a kitchen towel.

3. Add the rest of the ingredients to the batter and mix well.

4. To make the beguni, in a deep pan, add the oil and place the pan over high heat. It is important that the oil is hot, otherwise the coating will slide into the oil. Dip the brinjal slices into the batter and deep fry till they are puffed and crisp. They will only need 2–3 minutes on each side. You will need to flip them twice or thrice using a perforated spatula. Once done, take the beguni out of the oil and drain on a kitchen towel.

5. Serve with a hot cup of masala chai.

Egg Roll

I genuinely believe that I can measure my trips to Kolkata in egg rolls. I ate many versions of it – with chilli sauce, with tomato ketchup, with kasundi. But the ones I liked the most were the simple ones at Kusum Rolls in Park Street. A paratha seared well in butter, wrapped around fluffy eggs and lemon-soaked crunchy onions and green chilli resulted in the most soothing sequence of flavours.

And, I guess, that's what street food in India is all about – the charm of bold flavours mixed with comforting ones. The good part about these wraps is that they are easy to make since we only need a few ingredients to work with. The bad news is that your guests' faces will light up like bulbs as soon as they hear 'egg roll' and you'll end up making an infinite number of these. But since all you have to do is flip, fill and fold, you will have fun too.

I have Vikas, my friend and the head chef at Flury's, to thank for this recipe.

Prep time: 10 minutes | Cooking time: 10 minutes | Makes: 1

Ingredients

For the dough

1 cup all-purpose flour
2 tbsp vegetable oil
1 tsp nigella seeds
½ tsp sugar
1 tsp salt
¼ cup water

Method

1. To make the dough, put the all-purpose flour in a medium-sized bowl and add the oil, nigella seeds, sugar and salt. Mix well. Now, add water gradually to knead a stiff dough. Set aside to rest for 10 minutes.

2. In a bowl, add the sliced onions, green chilli, lemon juice and black salt. Mix well and set aside until required.

3. Whisk one egg and set aside until required.

For the stuffing
½ red onion, thinly sliced
½ green chilli, chopped
¼ tsp lemon juice
¼ tsp black salt
1 egg
Chaat masala, to sprinkle

4. To make the paratha for the roll, pinch off a medium-sized ball of the dough, roll it between your palms until smooth. With a rolling pin, roll out to a medium-sized disc of about 6 inches diameter.

5. Heat a medium-sized tawa, add 2 teaspoons of oil and then add the paratha. Cook for two minutes on each side, and then spread the egg on top. Let it cook for one minute and flip it. Let it cook for two more minutes, and then transfer it to a plate. Sprinkle the chaat masala and black salt using a tea strainer to ensure they are evenly spread.

6. Place the lemon-marinated onions and some green chillies in the centre of the parantha and roll it firmly. Wrap the bottom half of the roll with foil paper or butter paper.

Winter

Some of my fondest memories of winter from my childhood are of unrushed weekend mornings, when the four of us – Mummy, Papa, my sister and I – would squidge up inside a blanket and enjoy chai with some snacks. What we enjoyed the most, though, was the togetherness and conversations, with snacks providing the support structure. I remember secretly wishing for those moments to never get over. Now, whenever I wish to relive that familial warmth, all I have to do is to go into the kitchen and prepare the snacks we ate then, and I'm back under the blanket with my family.

Matar ki Kachori (Spicy Green Pea Puffs)

When I was a child, we waited for winters to arrive so that we could enjoy the sweet taste of fresh green peas (matar). As soon as they came into the market, Mummy would put them in everything – aloo matar, gobi matar, matar pulao, matar paneer, matar saag! You name a dish and it had peas!

By mid-January, we would feel like crying if we saw another green peas-plus-something dish on the dining table. But like all mothers, Mummy had a secret weapon up her sleeve. As soon as we started making faces at the word 'matar,' she converted the peas into her heavenly matar ki kachori, which none of us could get enough of. And even though there were only four of us at home, she never made the kachoris in small quantities. In fact, she always made a big kadhai of the stuffing and stored it in the refrigerator to ensure a continuous supply of kachoris with chai for the next few days. This is what I love most about home cooking – the generosity it comes with. I make my matar ki kachori the same way Mummy does: a crunchy kalonji crust filled with ginger-spiced, fennel-scented, mushy peas.

As good as these kachoris are, they are incomplete without the sharp contrast provided by the imli ki chutney. To prepare this chutney, just add all the ingredients into a saucepan and allow heat and time do their magic. Once ready, it stays fresh, even without the refrigerator, in an airtight jar for up to a month, and you can count on it to add an extra splash of flavours to your chillas, chaats, rolls, pakoras and barbecues whenever you want.

Prep time: 30 minutes | Cooking time: 30 minutes | Makes: 4–5

Ingredients

For the dough

1 cup all-purpose flour
1 tsp nigella seeds
¼ cup oil or maun
Salt, to taste
¼ cup water
Oil, for deep frying

Method

1. To make the dough, add the flour to a bowl, add the nigella seeds, oil and salt with a spoon. Mix them well. Gradually add water and knead into a stiff dough. Cover with a kitchen cloth and keep aside to rest for at least 30 minutes. There are two reasons we need to rest the dough: first, it will require less flour (parthan) to roll the kachoris, and second, they will puff up nicely.

For the tamarind chutney
½ cup tamarind pulp
1 cup water
1 cup jaggery, broken into small pieces
1 tsp black salt
1 tsp cumin powder
1 tsp red chilli powder
1½ tsp dried ginger powder (saunth)
Salt, to taste

For the stuffing
1 tbsp refined oil
1 tsp fennel seeds
A pinch of asafoetida powder (hing)
1 tsp green chilli, chopped
1 tsp grated ginger
1 tsp turmeric powder
1 tsp red chilli powder
1 tbsp coriander powder
1 tsp garam masala powder
1 cup green peas (defrost them if you are using frozen peas)
Salt, to taste
1 tbsp fresh coriander, chopped
½ tsp dried mango powder
½ tsp cumin powder

2. To make the chutney, add the tamarind pulp, water, jaggery, black salt, the spice powders and salt to a pan. Allow it to simmer for 20–30 minutes. Stir it once or twice, and let it continue to simmer. Once it is cooked, sieve it and collect it in a bowl. Adjust the seasoning and set aside until required.

3. To make the stuffing, heat oil in a pan, add the fennel seeds, asafoetida powder, chopped green chilli and grated ginger. Reduce the heat and add the turmeric, red chilli, coriander and garam masala powders. Then, add the peas and salt and mix well. Cover and cook for 3–4 minutes. Now, add the fresh chopped coriander, dried mango and cumin powders. Mix well. Using the back of a spatula, mash the peas coarsely. You can also add the peas to a mixer grinder and grind coarsely. Taste to adjust for salt and set aside until required.

4. To make the kachoris, place a small ball of dough between your palms and roll it until smooth. Now, using a rolling pin, roll the balls of dough into medium-sized circles and place the stuffing in the centre. Dip your finger in some water and run it over the edges of the disc. Bring the edges together to close it tightly. Repeat until all the kachoris have been made.

5. Heat the oil in a pan till medium hot, add the kachoris and fry on a low flame till golden brown. Flip them once or twice using a perforated spatula. Once done, take the kachoris out of oil and drain on a kitchen towel. Allow them to cool for 15–20 minutes before eating. Meanwhile you can prepare your masala chai.

6. Once cool, drizzle the tamarind chutney over the kachoris and enjoy with hot cup of masala chai.

Bread Rolls (Stuffed Bread Fritters)

Food is so intertwined with our feelings and emotions that recalling any particular taste brings back all the memories woven around it. In my case, these are visual memories. We all know that in the Hindu belief system, during the wedding ceremony, there is a ritual called the *kanyadaan*, which means to give away the daughter.

However, ironically, despite his best intentions and generous nature, my father could not come to terms with the idea of *kanyadaan*. So, when the time came to perform the *kanyadaan* during my wedding ceremony, he refused to do it. He said, 'I won't be party to this – she is and will remain my daughter for the rest of her life.' Thankfully, Panditji came up with a quick solution and the wedding ceremony was completed successfully, but this was one of the most memorable moments of my wedding due to the sense of protectiveness I felt from my father's words.

I got married on a cold January night, and all I was wearing was the *piri*, or the yellow sari traditionally worn by the bride for the ceremony. Right after the ceremony, sizzling hot bread rolls and chai were served, and they added to the warmth and comfort of Papa's words, and the taste stuck with me. Later, I called Mubarak, the caterer, to get the recipe. He has been feeding my family for more than 20 years now and, believe me, the flavours in his food bear the same meaning as his name – celebratory.

Prep time: 30 minutes | Cooking time: 15–20 minutes | Makes: 8–10

Ingredients

For the masala paste

½-inch piece of ginger

3–4 cloves of garlic

1 dried red chilli

2–3 black peppercorns

Method

1. To make the masala paste, add all the ingredients to a mixer jar, add ¼ cup of water and grind to a smooth paste. Take this out in a bowl and set it aside until required.

2. To make the stuffing, first mash the potatoes and set aside.

1 black cardamom
1 green cardamom
½-inch stick of cinnamon
1 tsp coriander seeds
¼ cup water

For the bread rolls
3 large potatoes, boiled and peeled
1 tbsp oil
1 tsp cumin seeds
1 onion, sliced
½ tsp turmeric powder
½ tsp red chilli powder
1 tsp garam masala powder
½ tsp dried mango powder
1 tsp coriander powder
½ cup green peas
2 tbsp water
Salt, to taste
6 slices of white bread
Oil, to deep fry

3. Heat oil in a pan, add the cumin seeds and let them crackle. Add the sliced onions and sauté till golden brown. Add the masala paste and sauté till the oil starts to separate, or for 3–4 minutes till the paste is fragrant. Add the turmeric, red chilli, garam masala, dried mango and coriander powders and sauté for 2 minutes. Add the peas and approximately 2 tablespoons of water, sprinkle some salt, cover and cook for 3–4 minutes. Add the mashed potatoes to the pan and mix well. Check for salt and let the stuffing cool down for a few minutes.

4. To make the rolls, cut the sides of the bread, give it a quick dip in the water. Place the stuffing in the centre and roll into the shape of a ball. Press tightly to make sure all the ends are properly closed. Repeat until all the bread rolls have been made.

5. To fry the bread rolls, heat the oil in a pan till very hot. Add the bread rolls in batches of 2–3 and fry till golden. You have to be really quick while frying the bread rolls as bread will start turning brown within seconds of touching the oil. Using a perforated spatula, take the rolls out of the oil and drain on a kitchen towel. Allow them to cool for 15–20 minutes before serving. You can make your masala chai during this time.

6. Serve with some ketchup or green chutney and masala chai.

Methi Mathri (Spiced and Fried Savoury Biscuits)

Every Diwali, two to three days before the big day, Mummy would make these crunchy methi mathris and promptly hide them in her wooden cabinet, a beautiful, heavily carved teakwood cabinet that matched the dining table she'd received from her parents on her wedding day. She also stored all her dining sets inside that cabinet, which is why it was strictly out of bounds to us. We usually never made any attempt to get into her cupboard, but all the rules fell by the wayside when it came to Mummy's methi mathris.

We would follow the trail created by the earthy aroma of the mathris, and we'd have almost finished them before Diwali arrived. The person who ate the most mathris was my Dadi (paternal grandmother). When she found the tin almost empty, Mummy would invariably ask, 'What will I serve the guests now?' With a cheeky grin on her face, Dadi would reply, 'On Diwali, no one goes back empty-handed. We can always feed them what they've brought!'

Dadi is no longer with us, but as I sit in my living room, eating these mathris with chai, I can feel the warmth of her love and the liveliness of those cheerful festivities from my childhood days all around me.

Prep time: 30 minutes | Cooking time: 30 minutes | Makes: 10–15

Ingredients

2 tsp crushed black pepper
1 tsp carom seeds
1 tsp fennel seeds
2 tsp coriander seeds
2 cups wholewheat flour
¼ cup semolina (suji)
2 tbsp dried fenugreek leaves (kasuri methi)

Method

1. In a small mixer jar, add the black pepper, carom seeds, fennel seeds and coriander seeds. Pulse them together once or twice to get a coarse spice powder. Set aside until required.

2. In a big bowl, add the wholewheat flour, semolina, spice powder, dried fenugreek leaves, oil/maun and salt. Mix well. Gradually add up to ¼ cup of water and knead a stiff dough. Cover the dough with a cotton cloth and leave it to rest for 30 minutes.

¼ cup maun or 3–4 tbsp of oil
Salt, to taste
Oil, deep frying

3. Then, pinch off small portion of the dough that is smaller than the size of a lime. Roll in between your palms to smoothen into a ball. Place it on your work surface, and then press it down into a roundel, which is at least 1-cm thick.

4. Heat enough oil in a pan to deep fry the mathris. To check if the oil is hot enough, drop a tiny portion of dough into the oil, and it should start floating on the surface. Gently slide the mathris into the oil and turn the heat down. Fry in batches of 3–4, flip them, once or twice using a perforated spatula. Fry till golden brown. Take the mathris out of the oil and drain on a kitchen towel. Allow them to cool for 15–20 minutes before serving. In the meanwhile, you can prepare your masala chai.

5. Enjoy the mathris doused in your favourite pickle with a cup of masala chai.

Bajra na Rotla no Choormo

(Pearl Millet Parathas Crumbled with Jaggery)

I love bajra for its intense earthiness and when you throw ghee and jaggery into the mix, it is pure nirvana for me. I first ate bajra na rotla no choormo, or bajre ki roti crumbled with soft jaggery, drizzled with smoking hot ghee and sprinkled with cardamom powder, at Megha Joshi's restaurant called Khichdi Garden in Andheri, Mumbai. Khichdi Garden is dedicated to authentic Gujarati food, and all the recipes come from Megha's family. To put it in Megha's words, 'These recipes are family heirlooms.'

We met during a shoot, and she invited me to dinner at Khichdi Gardens, where I ate much more than one person can possibly eat in a single sitting – the khichdi, the kadhi, the shak, the undhiyu, the kachoris, everything was simply amazing. But it was this comforting dish of bajra, ghee and jaggery, eaten with chai post dinner, that I wanted to bring to my kitchen and Megha was sweet enough to share the recipe.

My favourite thing about winters is cosying up inside a blanket. So I am always on the lookout for recipes that are easy to make, indulgingly delicious and easy to store – in short, recipes that don't keep me away from my blanket, books and chai for very long. This recipe checks all those boxes.

Prep time: 10 minutes | Cooking time: 10 minutes | Serves: 1

Ingredients

1 cup pearl millet (bajra) flour
1 tbsp + 1 tbsp ghee per rotla
¼ cup lukewarm water
¼ cup jaggery
½ tsp green cardamom powder
1 tsp toasted sesame seeds (optional)

Method

1. To make the rotla, put the pearl millet flour in a bowl, add ghee and mix well. Gradually add lukewarm water to knead a soft yet pliant dough. You will not need more than ¼ cup of water. Allow the dough to rest for a minimum of 20 minutes.

2. Take a pinch or a small portion of the dough between your fingers and roll between your palms to make a smooth ball. Now, sprinkle some flour on your work surface, and place the dough ball on it. Use a rolling pin to roll it into a medium-sized circle, and ignore the cracks on the edges.

3. Heat a tawa on a medium flame, add a teaspoon of ghee and then place the rotla on the tawa. Cook for 2–3 minutes, spread ghee on the top, flip the rotla and cook for 2–3 minutes. Take the rotla off the tawa and make more using the same method. Allow the rotlas to cool for minutes.

4. Break the rotlas into small pieces in a bowl, grate in the jaggery, add the cardamom powder and 1 tablespoon of ghee. Use your fingers to crumble everything together.

5. Sprinkle with some toasted sesame seeds and serve with a hot cup of masala chai.

Madhuri's Methi Theplas

(Spiced Fenugreek Flatbreads)

For a beautiful brief period in my life, I had the good fortune of experiencing Gujarati hospitality in all its glory. Madhuri, a very enthusiastic cook and a lovely person, from Kutch in Gujarat, lived right next door to me. Although she was younger than me, she behaved like my grandmother! Even before I realized it, I was like a family member. If I ever missed dinner with them, she would ask, 'Why didn't you come for dinner last night? I had to give the chapatis I made for you to the crows!'

On the days I stayed at home, beginning from the late afternoon till her husband arrived home from work, we would spend time indulging in chai, gossip and Gujju snacks! Of all the things she made, my favourite were her methi theplas. Her love and care towards me were overwhelmingly heart-warming – just like flavours of these theplas.

Prep time: 30 minutes | Cooking time: 30 minutes | Makes: 4

Ingredients

1 cup wholewheat flour
½ cup gram flour
2 tbsp yogurt
½ cup fresh fenugreek leaves
2 green chillies, finely chopped
½-inch piece ginger, grated
¼ bunch fresh coriander
1 tsp red chilli powder
½ tsp cumin seeds
2 tbsp + 2 tsp oil per thepla
Salt, to taste
Water

Method

1. Wash the fenugreek, pick out the leaves and then chop them. Chop the coriander and the green chillies. Set aside until required.

2. To make the theplas, in a bowl, add the wholewheat flour, gram flour, yogurt, fenugreek leaves, green chilli, ginger, chopped coriander, red chilli powder, cumin seeds, salt and 2 tablespoons of oil. Mix well, taste to check for salt. Gradually add water and knead into a soft dough. Let the dough rest for a minimum of 20 minutes.

3. Take a pinch or a lime-sized portion of dough and roll it between your palms to make a smooth ball. Dust your working surface with flour, place the dough ball on it, press it gently with fingers and using a rolling pin, roll it out into a medium-sized circle, around 6 cm in diameter.

4. Heat a tawa, add 1 teaspoon of oil and place the thepla on it. Cook for 2–3 minutes, lift it with a spatula and spread 1 more teaspoon of oil on the pan, and place the flipped thepla. Allow it to cook for 2–3 minutes and transfer it to a plate.

5. Enjoy with chutney, pickles and *mukka pyaaz* (an onion broken with your fist).

Aloo Tuk Chaat

(Double-fried Potatoes with Yogurt, Chutney and Pomegranate)

I have Chef Saransh Goila to thank for this recipe. We'd invited him and his mother on my TV show 'Amma Superstar' which aired on Zee Television. The concept of the show was to celebrate the support, inspiration and the beloved flavours imparted to our life by our mothers. Saransh's mother showed us her recipe for her famous butter paneer, which is also the recipe on which Saransh's success as an entrepreneur is built, and he showed us his recipe for this amazing aloo tuk.

While preparing the aloo tuk later at home, I wondered why the potatoes were being fried twice, but since it involved frying, I overlooked the extra step, and I thank god for that because the crunch it gives to the dish takes it to a whole new level. I also decided to go a step further and converted these crisp nuggets of sunshine into a chaat. Believe me, this is the best chaat in the world – paper crisp potatoes immersed in tangy tamarind chutney, punctuated with peppery chopped onions, sprinkled with black salt and studded with sweet pomegranate seeds – a plateful of food heaven. And since you are in food heaven, it's only right that you follow the time-honoured tradition of finishing with a cup of sweet chai after experiencing the sensation of chaat.

For this recipe, I prefer to use small round baby potatoes with a pinkish hue as they crisp up well because of their low moisture content. These baby potatoes show up in supermarkets only in the winter, and I tend to make this delightful recipe only then because nothing can replace the delight of seasonal veggies.

Prep time: 60 minutes | Cooking time: 15 minutes | Serves: 2

Ingredients

2 large potatoes, peeled
Oil, for deep frying
1 tsp black salt
1 tsp dried mango powder

Method

1. To make the aloo tuk, cut each potato into four quarters and wash them twice. Dry them using a kitchen towel.

½ tsp cumin powder
½ tsp red chilli powder
¼ tsp dry ginger powder

For the chaat
2 tbsp thick yogurt
1 tbsp tamarind chutney
1 tbsp green chutney
1 tbsp sev, for garnish
1 tbsp onion, chopped
1 tbsp pomegranate seeds
A pinch of black salt

2. Put the oil in a deep pan and heat it until very hot. Once the oil is hot, slide the potatoes in and fry on high heat for the first 2 minutes. Then, lower the heat to medium and fry till potatoes are on the verge of becoming golden. Remove from the oil using a perforated spatula and drain on a kitchen towel. Cool for 5 minutes or until you can handle them.

3. Now, place the fried potato on a chopping board or on a clean part of your kitchen counter. Using your palm, press each piece as gently as possible to flatten them. Then, return them to the hot oil and fry till they are golden. Remove from the oil and drain on a kitchen towel. Set aside until required.

4. In a large bowl, add all the dry spice powders and mix well. Toss in the crisp flattened potatoes, make sure each potato is coated properly with the masala. The traditional recipe of aloo tuk is now ready to be served.

5. To covert the tuk into a chaat, arrange them on a plate, and drizzle yogurt, tamarind chutney and green chutney over it. Sprinkle some sev, chopped onion, and pomegranate seeds. Put some black salt in a tea strainer and sprinkle over the chaat to ensure even distribution.

6. Enjoy with masala chai.

Sweet Potato Fries

This dish is a huge nostalgia trip for me. As I write this, I can see a scene playing out in front of my eyes, taking me back to every 14 January, or Makar Sankranti celebration of my life till the age of 12. Makar Sankranti was important to our elders because of its spiritual significance, but as children all we cared about was the Makar Sankranti Mela, which was filled with rides, traditional clay toys and food from nearby villages. At that point, we were living in Shahdol, my birthplace and a small town in the heart of Madhya Pradesh, so we were surrounded by villages and their rustic flavours and traditions. After finishing with the rides and spending most of the year's saving on toys, my sister and I would fight over which stall to stop at first, and the one with sweet potato fries always won.

The crisp, fried golden sweet potatoes, full of sweet and salty flavours, were our favourites, and we always bought one cone for each of us. We'd request the lady selling the fries to sprinkle some extra masala on top of our fries. We could never finish our fries because the portion was usually huge, and there were too many other stalls to stop at! We'd bring them home and enjoy them with chai the next day.

It has been many years since I last visited a mela on Makar Sankranti – in fact, I count myself lucky if I have the time and energy to make some black sesame laddoos (kale til ke laddoo, a traditional sweet for Makar Sankranti). But the one thing I always do is make sweet potato fries every 14 January since they are easy to make. As soon as I take a bite, sitting in the comfort of my living room, I can hear the creaky noise of the *rahat* (a wooden manually operated ride), feel the thrumming of the whole town coming together, and taste that earthiness from the layer of dust on top of every snack we used to eat.

Prep time: 5 minutes | Cooking time: 15 minutes | Serves: 2

Ingredients
Water, to boil
2 sweet potatoes
Oil, for deep frying

For the masala mix
1 tsp black salt
½ tsp dry mango powder
¼ tsp cumin powder
⅛ tsp coriander powder
½ tsp red chilli powder
¼ tsp dry ginger powder
⅛ tsp cinnamon powder
Salt, to taste

Method

1. To make the fries, first put water in a large, deep pan and place it on the stove to boil. Peel the sweet potatoes and wash them. Chop them into a matchstick-like shape: first cut them in ½-inch thick rounds, then slice each round vertically into a stick of ½-inch thickness. Add the chopped sweet potatoes to the boiling water and let them boil for 2 minutes. Drain them and dry them with a kitchen towel.

2. Heat the oil in a pan. Add the dried sweet potato sticks and fry till they are golden brown. Using a perforated spatula, transfer the fries to a plate lined with absorbent paper.

3. Add all the masalas to a bowl and mix well. Toss in the fries, making sure each fry is well coated in masala.

4. Enjoy with a hot cup of masala chai.

Kerala Golden Sev (Deep-fried Rice Pastry)

My father is an avid traveller – in fact, according to my grandmother, he exhausted his first salary on a voyage to Lakshadweep. So, it did not come as a big surprise to his family when he announced a tour of south India the day after his wedding. It was basically their honeymoon, but in those days, they were too shy to call it that. But it was a big surprise for the 20-year-old girl who had never been on a train before – my mother. As scared as she was, it did not discourage her from asking the Malayali family with whom they shared their train compartment for the recipe of this delicious sev. Mummy could not speak English, and her new friend did not speak much Hindi, but they connected over this simple dish.

For so many years, my mother, my sister and I have spent so many afternoons munching on this sev and sipping sweet masala chai. We have laughed, gossiped and argued around it. What I miss most about being away from them is our chai hour – a perfect, peaceful hour. This sev is not that difficult to make and its crunchy crumbliness loves chai very much.

Using cream instead of water to knead the dough makes the sev softer and enhances its shelf life. You can easily store it for two weeks in an airtight container – carrying a container of this sev on a trip or a vacation can make life very convenient.

Prep time: 5 minutes | Cooking time: 15 minutes | Serves: 2

Ingredients

1 kg rice
250 gm split black lentils (split urad dal)
2 tsp carom seeds

Method

1. Wash the rice and dal two to three times and drain completely. Spread it on a cloth and dry in the shade. As soon as the moisture is gone, transfer to a blender and grind to a fine powder.

1 tsp garam masala powder
1 tsp black pepper powder
1 cup fresh cream (malai)
1–2 tbsp milk, if required
Salt, to taste
Oil, for deep frying

2. Empty the powder in a large mixing bowl. Add the carom seeds, garam masala powder and black pepper. Gradually add the cream and keep stirring to form a dough. In case you feel the dough is dry, add a tablespoon or two of milk. Cover it and set aside for 2 hours.

3. Heat the oil in a deep pan over medium heat.

4. Grease the insides of a piping bag or the walls of a sev-making press, whichever you are using, with oil. Transfer the prepared dough to a piping bag with a single-hole nozzle or to the sev-making press. Hold the piping bag, or the sev machine, over the pan and press down gently to let the dough drip in the hot oil. As soon as there's no more space inside the wok, put the piping bag down. And use a perforated spatula to flip the sev while frying. Fry till golden brown. Use the spatula to remove the sev from the pan and drain the extra oil on absorbent paper. Store in an airtight container.

5. Enjoy with a cup of masala chai.

Summer

During summers it makes sense to consume drinks that are cold, but I for one find it impossible to abandon my cup of tea no matter how hot the weather gets. Having said that, I too need respite from the heat, and for that I maintain a balance by pairing my cup of tea with a mild and refreshing snack rather than a hot and spicy one. These are the recipes you will find in this section.

Mungaudi (Yellow Moong Dal Fritters/Lentil Fritters)

Growing up in Bhopal, every evening after college, various *tapris*, or informal tea stalls, used to be the favourite hangout spot for me and my friends. What I loved about some of these *tapris* was the delicious mungaudi they served. I don't feel like going out every evening these days, I like the cosy comfort of my home much better. But I do often feel like enjoying crisp, gingery mungaudis with my rich sweet chai every evening.

Prep time: 20 minutes | Cooking time: 15 minutes | Serves: 2

Ingredients

200 gm split moong beans (moong dal)
2 tsp grated ginger
1 medium-sized onion, finely chopped
1 tsp green chilli, chopped
1 tbsp fresh coriander, chopped
½ tsp red chilli powder
¼ tsp turmeric powder
½ tsp cumin powder
A pinch of asafoetida
Salt, to taste
Oil, for deep frying

Method

1. Soak the moong beans for 4–5 hours or overnight. Drain and grind into a coarse paste. In a big bowl, add the moong bean paste and all the rest of the ingredients except the oil. Mix well. Taste and adjust seasoning if required.

2. Heat the oil in a wok over medium heat. Add a tablespoon of the batter to the hot oil and fry over medium heat till golden brown and crisp.

3. Serve with your favourite chutney and a cup of chai.

Bhurji-Pav

(Buns Topped With Spicy Scrambled Eggs and Melted Cheese)

To me, bhurji–pav means laid-back Sunday mornings in the hostel mess in Mumbai University, where a bunch of hungry girls would gather around for conversations over gallons of sweet chai and eggs. Just imagine melted cheese trickling through the layers of turmeric-spiced scrambled eggs (anda bhurji), sitting on top of a butter-browned bun, and you will be able to understand the gratifying complexity of flavours I am talking about here. This is the kind of recipe that slows you down, pacifies you, makes you feel the relaxing magic of the weekend.

Prep time: 10 minutes | Cooking time: 20–30 minutes | Serves: 4

Ingredients

2 tbsp oil
½ tsp cumin seeds
1 large onion, chopped
1 tsp green chilli, chopped
1 tsp ginger, grated
½ tsp red chilli powder
½ tsp turmeric powder
2 tbsp coriander, chopped
6 eggs, whisked
Salt, to taste
2 tbsp butter
4 buns (pav)
4 tbsp grated cheese
4 cheese slices

Method

1. Heat the oil in a pan, add cumin seeds and let them crackle. Add the onion and sauté till pink. Add the green chilli, ginger, spice powders and coriander. Cook for 1 minute.

2. Add the eggs, sprinkle some salt to taste and start stirring till the eggs are cooked. Set aside until required.

3. Heat a medium-sized shallow pan and spread 1 tablespoon of butter on it. Add two pavs or buns and sear till golden brown and crisp. Take the pan off the heat and place a slice of cheese on each bun and top with the scrambled egg. Then, top with some grated cheese. Cover the pan with a lid and place back on the heat but on the lowest setting. Cook till cheese is melted.

4. Alternatively, preheat an oven to 200 degrees Celsius. Place the browned buns on a baking tray, top off with cheese slices, scrambled egg and grated cheese. Place under the grill and cook till cheese is melted and brown.

Caramelized Onions and Hung Yogurt Sandwich

This is my mother-in-law's recipe, and I love it because it is a generous, fulfilling snack that pairs well with chai or coffee and is easy to make. It is, in effect, a very cordial alignment of toasted bread, velvety, sweet, caramelized onions and creamy yogurt.

I often prepare the caramelized onions a day or two before I am planning to make these beauties. And I always make some extra as they store well in the refrigerator. (It also ensures I am only a few minutes away from a gorgeous curry or stew.) Also, in case hung curd feels like a bit too much by all means go for cream cheese, because it too works wonderfully well.

Prep time: 30 minutes | Cooking time: 10 minutes | Makes: 4

Ingredients

1 cup full-fat yogurt
2 tbsp refined oil
3 large onions, thinly sliced
Salt, to taste
1 tsp butter, for the onions
1 tsp butter, for the bread
4 slices of bread (of your choice)
1 tbsp coriander leaves, finely chopped

Method

1. To make the hung curd, put the yogurt in a muslin cloth, tie it and let the whey drip for a minimum of 2 hours. An easier way to do this is to put the yogurt in a large strainer and balance it on top of a bowl. The water will drain away in 10–12 minutes.

2. To make the caramelized onions, heat 2 tablespoons of oil in a medium-sized shallow pan. Add the sliced onions, sprinkle some salt and cook them gently, stirring over very low heat till they are deep brown. Once they turn brown, add 1 teaspoon of butter and let it melt. Then, transfer them to a bowl and let them cool for 15–20 minutes.

3. Heat a teaspoon of butter on a tawa and place 2 slices of breads on it and sear on a low flame till it turns brown. Place them on a plate and let them cool for 2 minutes.

4. Spread the hung yogurt, top it with the caramelized onions and coriander leaves.

5. Serve with a hot cup of tea.

Shrewsbury Biscuits

One of the legends of Pune's vibrant food scene is the Kayani Bakery, most famous for their Shrewsbury biscuits. These biscuits are rich, buttery and subtly sweet – everything a chai loves. In Pune, they often eat these biscuits with the famous Amrutulya chai, which is much like a masala chai.

At the Kayani Bakery, they guard their recipes with their lives, and all my attempts to get an authentic recipe were unsuccessful. My attempt to bake these biscuits at home by guessing the recipe based on taste, though, was super successful.

Prep time: 20 minutes | Baking time: 10–12 minutes | Makes: 15

Ingredients

100 gm butter
75 gm sugar
1 large egg
1 tsp vanilla essence
200 gm all-purpose flour
50 gm cashew nuts, roasted
1–2 tbsp milk
Caster sugar, for sprinkling

Method

1. In a large bowl, cream the butter and sugar together until light and fluffy. Whisk in the egg and vanilla and combine well. Add the flour and cashew nuts and mix well. Knead into a soft dough by gradually adding the milk. Cover with cling film and cool the dough inside the refrigerator for 20 minutes.

2. Preheat the oven to 200 degrees Celsius. Lightly grease and line a baking tray with baking parchment.

3. Take the dough out of the refrigerator and using a rolling pin, roll it out into a thin sheet about ½-cm thick. Using a small cookie cutter, cut out the biscuits and gently place them on the baking tray. Sprinkle the sugar over each biscuit and bake for 10–12 minutes.

4. Take the tray out of the oven and leave the biscuits on the baking tray for 5 minutes. Then, transfer to a cooling rack to cool completely.

Jeera Biscuits

There are very few other delights in the world as satisfying as baking your own biscuits and enjoying their light crunch while they are still slightly hot. A jar of these crisp one-step, two-ingredient biscuits is a comforting sight, especially early in the morning. One glimpse of these simple salted biscuits and I feel like a cup of chai.

I have made these linear, but you can shape into twists if you wish to, but why complicate it when you can keep things straight? Plus, twisting each biscuit takes extra effort and chai time is all about unwinding.

Prep time: 5 minutes | Baking time: 20–25 minutes | Makes: 15–20

Ingredients

1 sheet of puff pastry

1 tbsp milk

1 cup grated processed cheese

1 tbsp cumin seeds

Method

1. Prepare a medium-sized cookie tray by lining it with baking parchment.

2. If you are using a slab of puff pastry, dust your work surface with flour, place the puff pastry on it and roll it out into a 3–4-mm-thick rectangle. Place the puff pastry on top of the baking tray and let it rest it in the refrigerator for 30 minutes. Once rested, take the pastry out and place it on a lightly dusted work surface. If you are using a puff pastry sheet, ignore this step.

3. Brush the top of the puff pastry sheet with milk, sprinkle the cheese and cumin seeds on top and press it down gently with your hands so that it sticks. Cut 3-mm-wide strips of the pastry and rest them in the refrigerator for 30 minutes. Preheat the oven to 180 degrees Celsius for at least 20 minutes while the pastry is resting.

4. Once rested, take the tray out of the refrigerator and place it inside the oven. Bake for 20–25 minutes or until the biscuits are golden. Cool for 10 minutes before serving.

5. Make a cup of chai and enjoy with jeera biscuits.

Nimki/Namak Paare (Crunchy Fried Pastry)

Festivals present a fabulous opportunity to relive the familiar comforts of childhood, and for me that familiarity comes mostly from home-cooked meals. When I think of how we celebrated Holi during my childhood, the first thing that comes to mind is nimki – the aroma of hot oil wafting out of the kitchen, announcing the frying of copious quantities of these delights. My mother always made sure that there was a steady supply of 'something to eat' with chai for the guests who constantly stopped by.

Honestly, making the dough by hand is a bit of an effort. But on the other side of it lies the irresistible crunch of nimki flowing out of the jar for days to come. I love nimki for their plain, salty crunch infused with earthiness of nigella seeds. Whenever I make them now, they pair incredibly well, in my memory and in present, with a cup of sweet masala chai.

Prep time: 20 minutes | Cooking time: 30 minutes | Makes: 30–40

Ingredients

2 cups all-purpose flour
¼ cup ghee
1 tbsp nigella seeds
1 tsp carom seeds
Salt, to taste
1 cup lukewarm water, to knead with
Oil, for deep frying

Method

1. To make the nimkis, put the flour, ghee, nigella seeds, carom seeds and salt in a bowl. Mix everything together with your hands and taste to check for salt.

2. Now, pour in the lukewarm water, bit by bit, to knead a stiff dough. You may not need all of the water. Cover the dough with a wet towel and set aside for 20 minutes.

3. Divide the dough in two equal parts. Take one ball and roll it out to a 1-cm thick sheet. Using a knife, cut the sheet vertically then horizontally. We are looking for matchstick-shaped cut-outs that are a maximum of 3 inches long and 1 centimetre wide. Separate them and fry in hot oil till golden.

4. Serve with a cup of chai but sometimes for that extra oomph, I put the nimkis on a serving plate and mix them with some finely chopped onions, lemon juice and fried green chillies.

Cheese Biscuits

Think of these biscuits as a baked, creamy and more crumbly version of nimki. I learned of this recipe during my culinary course in Italy, and it immediately became one of my favourites. The creamy saltiness and light crunch of these biscuits are the perfect accompaniment for rich, sweet chai.

Prep time: 20 minutes | Cooking time: 15–20 minutes | Makes: 10–15

Ingredients

100 gm butter
1 large egg yolk
200 gm processed cheese, grated
140 gm all-purpose flour
1 tbsp carom seeds
A pinch of salt

Method

1. In a large bowl, beat the butter until pale. Whisk in the egg yolk and then gently fold in the cheese. Add the flour, carom seeds and salt. Fold to make a soft dough, and then flatten it to form a thick disc. Wrap this in cling film and place in the refrigerator for at least 30 minutes.

2. Preheat the oven to 200 degrees Celsius and prepare a baking tray by lining its base with baking parchment.

3. Once the dough is rested, dust the work surface with flour and roll it out into ½-cm-thick sheet.

4. Using a cookie cutter, cut into medium-sized circles or whatever shape you fancy and place in the baking tray. Put the tray inside the oven and bake for 15–20 minutes. Remove from the oven and transfer to a cooling rack or a ceramic plate and leave to cool completely.

5. To serve, you can make canapes with these biscuits. Place a slice of tomato and basil on top and tuck in. You can use any toppings you like such as pesto and tomato, chutney and cucumber, mayonnaise and a slice of boiled egg, etc.

Bhuna Paneer Roll

In the narrow streets of Bhopal's 10 Number Market is a snack shop popularly known across Bhopal as Cycle Soupwala Shop since it is owned by a person who started his journey by selling hot tomato soup from the back of his cycle – a classic rags-to-riches story. This shop sells the best paneer kathi rolls in the world – clusters of spicy, charred paneer doused in tandoori masala and soaked in refreshing chutney. They are addictive. When I am away from Bhopal, it is this paneer kathi roll that I miss the most. Although it is not easy to reproduce the smoky, chargrilled flavours of a hot tandoor at home, this recipe comes close to the original.

Prep time: 30 minutes | Cooking time: 30 minutes | Makes: 4

Ingredients

For the kathi roll

1 tsp garam masala powder
A pinch of chaat masala powder
1 tsp red chilli powder
1 tsp ginger-garlic paste
1 tsp mustard oil
Juice of ½ lime
½ tsp black salt
Salt, to taste
2 tbsp hung yogurt
1 cup paneer, cubed
½ cup onion, cut in squares
2 tsp green chutney
2 tortillas or leftover rotis or parathas

Method

1. Preheat the oven to 220 degrees Celsius.

2. To make the paneer filling, in a large bowl, add all the dry spice powders, ginger-garlic paste, mustard oil, lime juice, both the salts and hung yogurt. Mix well. Add the paneer and onion to the marinade and make sure they are coated well.

3. Switch on the grill in the oven, and thread the marinated pieces of paneer on a skewer, alternating with onions. Then, place the skewers on a baking tray or balance the skewers on the edges of the baking tray so that the paneer does not touch the surface of the tray. Place the tray under the grill till the paneer is charred. Use a fork to transfer the paneer from the skewers into a bowl.

For the green chutney
1 cup coriander leaves
½ cup mint leaves
2 green chillies
1 clove of garlic
½-inch piece of ginger
⅛ tsp black salt
A pinch of cumin powder
Salt, to taste

4. Alternatively, you can also heat a thick-bottomed pan, a griddle pan or a cast iron pan and place the marinated pieces of paneer on it, making sure there is space between each piece. Cook on high heat till the paneer is charred. Then, using a flat spatula, transfer them to a plate or a bowl.

5. While the paneer is being grilled, prepare the chutney. Add all the ingredients for the chutney to a blender jar and blitz it up. Transfer to a bowl until required.

6. To make the kathi roll, heat a tawa and place a roti or paratha on the pan and warm it roughly for a minute on each side. Place the paratha on a plate, arrange the pieces of paneer and onion in the centre and drizzle with the green chutney. Fold to close it, and for the ease of eating, wrap the bottom half of the roll in foil.

Assam Orthodox

The word 'orthodox' normally means something that conforms to old methods. However, in the tea world, the term refers to the way tea is processed. Centuries ago, when the tribes of the hills of Assam started making tea, they would roll the tea leaves between their palms to bruise them gently, and not crush them, to get the natural juices out. These days, many tea companies in Assam devote a certain percentage of the harvest to be processed using the orthodox method. The same age-old, gentle hand-rolling method is imitated by machines, and this tea is known as orthodox.

The gentle rolling of the orthodox method allows the leaf to remain whole, resulting in a subtle and soothing flavour as compared to CTC. The orthodox method also involves a minimum amount of heat and friction from the machine, ensuring the full measure of natural antioxidants which makes Assam Orthodox a premium and highly sought-after tea. I always associate Assam Orthodox with a sense of fun. When I returned after completing my tea research, my best friend Hanine, who is equally passionate about tea, came to visit. She had made and brought my favourite snack out of all the dishes she makes, her semolina cake, and I had brewed some tea. She took one sip and asked me what tea we were drinking. I told her that it was Assam Orthodox, and she instantly asked, 'What? The tea is Christian?' We laughed our hearts out.

Basbousa (Semolina Cake)

This is one of my favourite cakes in the world – I love the sugar syrup-soaked sponge interspersed with the crumbliness of semolina. The fact that this recipe comes from my best friend Hanine adds greatly to the comfort I derive from this cake because she is the only person I turn to for peace, fun and strength.

The mild sweetness of this cake pairs very well with the mellow flavours of Assam Orthodox. Sometimes, Hanine and I add a few fresh mint leaves to our Assam Orthodox tea while it is brewing and enjoy the cooling effects of mint tea after lunch or on summer evenings.

Prep time: 20 minutes | Baking time: 20 minutes | Serves: 8–10

Ingredients

Butter, to grease
4 large eggs
100 gm sugar
100 ml sunflower oil
(or any neutral oil)
60 ml milk
1 tsp vanilla extract
300 gm semolina
80 gm all-purpose flour
½ tbsp baking powder

Method

1. Preheat the oven to 180 degrees Celsius. Grease a 23-cm springform pan with butter and line the base with baking parchment.

2. In a large bowl, using a handheld whisk or an electric whisk, whisk the eggs until frothy. Whisk in the sugar, oil, milk and vanilla extract. Gently fold in the semolina, flour and baking powder. Tip the batter into the springform pan and bake at 180 degrees Celsius for 20 minutes.

3. To make the syrup, in a saucepan, add the sugar and water and boil till sugar is melted. Keep stirring, turn down the heat and simmer for 4–5 minutes. Add the orange juice and rose water. Mix well. Let it simmer for one more minute and then take it off the heat. Set aside until required.

For the syrup
125 gm sugar
350 ml water
2 tbsp orange juice or juice of 1 orange
A few rose petals or a few drops rose water

Decoration (optional)
¼ cup Greek yogurt
1 tsp icing sugar
A few dried rose petals or 1 tsp rose water
½ cup pistachios, chopped

4. Take the cake out of the oven and place it on top of a cooling rack, without demoulding it. Use a skewer to poke holes on the surface of the cake. Pour the syrup over the cake and let the cake absorb it. Let it stand for at least 60 minutes.

5. To decorate the cake, place the yogurt, rose water and icing sugar in a small bowl. Use a fork to gently mix them together. Spread the yogurt mixture on top of the cake and sprinkle some pistachios. Place the cake on the serving platter and serve.

Raisin Bread

'Breadmaking is one of those almost hypnotic businesses, like a dance from some ancient ceremony. It leaves you filled with one of the world's sweetest smells... there is no chiropractic treatment, no yoga exercise, no hour of meditation in a music-throbbing chapel that will leave you emptier of bad thoughts than this ceremony of making bread,' writes M.F.K. Fisher, the iconic American food writer, in her book *How to Cook a Wolf.*

The essence of what Fisher is saying is something that I have experienced while baking this bread, or for that matter any bread. The process of bread-making is so natural to us humans – all that mixing, kneading and watching it rise in the oven – that we can let our hands take over our minds and not think and simply be. I find that the mind is able to decompress and rid itself what does not serve it well during this process. And at the end, you have a product that has been nourishing mankind for millennia, giving you a deep sense of divine satisfaction.

This bread has a permanent place at my breakfast table as it is a pleasure to make it and stays in the refrigerator for weeks – although you may finish it much sooner! I love its bejewelled texture interwoven with the comforting notes of musky spices. The flavours of my raisin bread simply adorn the robustness of Assam Orthodox.

Prep time: 30 minutes | Baking time: 30 minutes | Serves: 6–8

Ingredients

200 gm raisins
50 ml rum or orange juice
75 ml lukewarm milk
1 large egg
250 gm all-purpose flour
25 gm brown sugar
½ tsp or 3.5 gm dried yeast

Method

1. Soak the raisins in rum overnight.

2. Grease an 8x4x3-inch loaf tin with butter and line the base with baking parchment. Set aside until required.

3. In a jug add milk and egg, whisk together and set aside until required.

½ tsp allspice powder
75 gm salted butter, cubed + butter, to grease
1 tsp almond essence
Zest and juice of 1 lemon
½ tsp dried ginger
½ tsp ground cinnamon
50 gm pistachios, chopped
2 tbsp icing sugar (optional)

4. In a large mixing bowl, add the flour, sugar and yeast. Add all the spices (allspice powder, dried ginger, ground cinnamon), butter, almond essence, zest and juice of lemon, pistachios and rum-soaked raisins. Use a spatula to mix everything together.

5. Now knead everything into a dough, by gradually adding the milk and egg mixture into the flour mixture. It will be a very soft dough. If you have one, I recommend using the stand mixer for this dough. Once everything comes together, apply a bit of oil to your working surface and on your palms. Turn the dough on the working surface and fold for 3–4 minutes. Then, place in a well-oiled bowl and cover with a tea towel. Rest for a minimum of 40 minutes.

6. Once the dough is rested, sprinkle some flour on your working surface, turn the dough on it and fold it into a loaf. Place the loaf on a baking tray and cover with a tea towel. Allow it to rise for one hour.

7. Preheat the oven to 220 degrees Celsius for 20 minutes. Place the tray in the oven and bake for 30 minutes.

8. Let the bread cool off for 20 minutes, dust with icing sugar, slice and serve with a hot cup of Assam Orthodox.

Kesar and Kishmish Muffins

(Saffron and Raisin Muffins)

I would not have known the pleasures of the flavours of saffron, rose and raisins baked together in a muffin if it had not been for Ayeh, my Iranian friend and neighbour. For her, it is not possible to cook anything without using saffron. Be it rice preparations, koftas, kebabs, curries and most of all desserts – all her food uses saffron!

'I cherish traditions, but I also love creating something new,' says Ayeh. These muffins are her interpretation of the famous Irani biscuits, shereeni kesmeshi. I must say that I would have baked the biscuits just for how beautifully poetic the name is. These muffins became my instant favourite as they have a very cosy feel with their golden texture and all the goodness of saffron with raisins snuggled tightly inside it.

The fulfilling nature of these muffins makes for a wonderful breakfast but since they are subtly sweet, I sometimes warm them slightly for 10 seconds or so in the microwave, spread some butter over them and drizzle some honey or maple syrup. It is my idea of food heaven!

To ensure that muffins are light and fluffy, there is just one rule to follow – do not overwork the batter. Fold in everything together with a very gentle hand. Please feel free to add any nuts of your choice like pistachio or cashew nuts, I am sure it will only bring a beautiful crunch.

Prep time: 20 minutes | Baking time: 20 minutes | Makes: 12

Ingredients

250 gm raisins
2 tsp saffron strands
2 tsp rose water
200 ml buttermilk
75 gm butter, salted

Method

1. Preheat the oven to 200 degrees Celsius. Line a muffin tray with 12 paper cases.

2. Roughly chop the raisins and set aside. Add saffron and rose water to the buttermilk and set aside.

75 gm caster sugar
1 large egg
200 gm all-purpose flour
2 tsp baking powder
½ tsp bicarbonate of soda
1½ tbsp dried rose petals

3. Put the butter and sugar in a large mixing bowl and using a handheld or an electric whisk, whisk together into a smooth fluffy mixture. Add the egg and whisk well. Now whisk in the buttermilk mixture.

4. In a separate bowl, sift the flour, baking powder and bicarbonate of soda. Then, fold in the chopped up raisins and rose petals. Gently fold in the dry ingredients into the wet ingredients. Spoon the batter into the muffin cases and bake for 20 minutes, by that time they will have risen and will be golden and cooked.

5. Leave them in the tray for 5 minutes, and then cool for at least 10 minutes before serving.

Ginger and Honey Cake

I have a great deal of nostalgic love for this combination of flavours. As a child, whenever we had a cough, Mummy would mix dried ginger with honey and give it to us before we went to bed. Comforted by the pungent warmth of ginger and the sweet kiss of honey, our throats would almost magically be healed by the next morning. Years later, sitting in my favourite café in Bhopal, Café Chino, I found the same comforting flavours in this cake, and I simply could not leave without asking for the recipe.

This is my favourite cake to bake, especially when I know that I have some time to myself. Being glued to the sofa, beside my favourite window, in the company of my favourite author, comforted by the familiar flavours of this ginger and honey cake and a hot cup of Assam Orthodox is what defines bliss for me.

Simmering the liquid ingredients separately is an important step as it brings the density of the final product down and helps retain the light and crumbly texture of the cake.

Prep time: 30 minutes | Baking time: 50–60 minutes | Serves: 6–8

Ingredients

100 gm butter
100 gm caster sugar
200 gm honey
200 ml milk
1 tbsp ground ginger
1 tsp allspice powder
2 eggs, beaten
225 gm all-purpose flour

Method

1. Preheat the oven to 180 degrees Celsius. Grease an 8x4x3-inch loaf tin with butter and line the base of with baking parchment.

2. Place butter, sugar and honey in a saucepan on a low flame and simmer it gently to let the butter melt. Set it aside and let it cool for 5–6 minutes. Whisk in milk, ground ginger, allspice powder. Add the eggs one at a time. Then, fold in the chopped walnuts.

3. In a separate bowl, sift in flour, baking powder and bicarbonate of soda. Now, gently fold the wet ingredients into the dry ingredients.

3 tsp baking powder
1 tsp bicarbonate of soda
50 gm walnuts, roughly chopped

4. Add the batter into the baking tin and bake for 50–60 minutes, or till a skewer inserted in the middle comes out clean. Place the tin on a cooling rack and let it cool in the tin for 15 minutes. Then to unmould it, place a plate on top of the loaf tin and gently flip it. Tap the bottom of the loaf tin all over with your fingers to ensure even loosening of the cake.

5. Brush the top with honey, and allow it to rest for 10 minutes. Slice and serve warm.

Dhokla

During my childhood, while spending a summer vacation in Ahmedabad, Gujarat, my family and I tasted the most delicious snack at one of my father's friend's houses – it was dhokla. We liked it so much that each one of us shamelessly reached out for 4 or 5 helpings. Ignoring her fear of embarrassing herself and us, my mother walked up to the lady of the house and pleaded for the recipe. Below you will find that time-tested recipe. Dhoklas taste immensely earthy, are gluten free, vegan and very easy to make.

Prep time: 15 minutes | Cooking time: 15–20 minutes | Makes: 4–5

Ingredients

1 cup split chickpeas (chana dal)
1 cup rice
1 tbsp grated ginger
1 tbsp green chilli, chopped
Salt, to taste
A pinch of asafoetida
1/2 tsp turmeric

For tempering

2 tsp oil
1 tsp mustard seeds
1 tsp cumin
4-5 curry leaves

Method

1. Soak the split chickpeas and rice overnight.

2. Drain the water and grind the mixture to a paste. Let it ferment for 5–6 hours and add grated ginger, green chilli, salt, asafoetida and cumin. Mix all the ingredients well.

3. Add the batter to the steamer and steam for 15–20 minutes.

4. As soon as the dhokla is done, take the tray out of the steamer and let it rest for 15 minutes. Once it cools down, cut the dhokla into square pieces.

5. To prepare the tempering, heat oil in a pan. Add mustard seeds and cumin to the pan and allow them to crackle. Then add the curry leaves and let them crisp up.

6. Pour this super earthy tempering mix on top of the dhokla and enjoy with tea.

Thai Corn Fritters

Tea parties are all about sharing light-hearted conversations and lovely snacks with your friends and family, and these corn fritters are perfect for the occasion. Sweet and chewy corn fritters paired with the woodsy flavours of Assam Orthodox tea is everything you need for time well spent with your loved ones. The secret to making the perfect fritters lies in ensuring that the quantity of batter is one-third the quantity of the other ingredients used.

Prep time: 10 minutes | Cooking time: 15–20 minutes | Makes: 15–20

Ingredients

500 gm fresh or frozen corn
3 spring onions, chopped
1 large red chilli, chopped
1 tsp grated ginger
2 tbsp coriander, chopped
Juice of 1 lime
1 tsp soy sauce
1 tsp sesame seed oil
Black salt, to taste
1 large egg
90 gm all-purpose flour
½ tsp baking powder
4 tbsp coconut milk
Oil, to fry

Method

1. To make the batter, add flour, black salt and baking powder to a medium-sized mixing bowl. Gradually pour in coconut milk while whisking to make a smooth batter and then add the oil.

2. If you need to defrost the corn, boil water in a saucepan and add the corn. Let it boil for 4-5 minutes and then drain.

3. Mix the corn into the bowl containing the batter.

4. Add chopped spring onion, red chilli, grated ginger, coriander, lime juice, soy sauce, sesame seed oil, salt, egg, all-purpose flour, baking powder. Mix everything together.

5. Now, heat oil in a non-stick pan. Add a spoonful of corn batter to the pan to make the fritters. Fry for 3 to 4 minutes on each side. Remove the fritters from the pan and serve with some ketchup.

English Breakfast Tea

According to Helen Saberi's book, *Tea: A Global History*, 'By the middle of the eighteenth-century tea-drinking had spread to the middle classes and replaced ale for breakfast and gin at other times of the day. As coffee drinking declined, tea became Britain's most popular beverage.' And in *Darjeeling: A History of the World's Greatest Tea*, Jeff Koehler writes, 'instead of sending our ships to Canton for our Tea, we shall send them to Calcutta for the rich and well-flavoured teas of Assam, Chachar, Darjeeling-Kumaon, other tea-growing districts.'

Within four decades of starting commercial tea production in India, by 1888, Britain had finally begun to import more tea from India than China. It was an 'imperial dream come true'.

I mention these quotes here to ascertain two facts. One, how much England depended on tea and, two, how happy they were to find it in India. From there, it was only a matter of time until strong Assamese black tea became as famous as the English Breakfast Tea. It has a rich and robust flavour profile with a woody aroma as a result of being a beautiful blend of Assam Orthodox and CTC.

Although English Breakfast is meant to be diluted with milk and sugar, I prefer it without any. But what I do like to do with black tea is contrasting its rich flavours with some sweet snacks and these are my favourite pairings.

Pumpkin Bread

Pumpkin bread – the name itself induces a festive spirit. The sweet, buttery flavour of pumpkin punctuated by the heat of musky spices makes the bread perfect for teatime.

Prep time: 20 minutes | Baking time: 50 minutes | Serves: 8–10

Ingredients

For the cake

125 gm pumpkin puree
or 1 medium-sized pumpkin
3 large eggs
65 gm brown sugar
250 gm almond flour
2 tsp allspice powder
1 tsp ground cinnamon
¼ tsp grated nutmeg
1 tsp bicarbonate of soda
2 tsp baking powder
60 ml oil

Method

1. You can buy a can of pumpkin puree from the market, but if you want to prepare your own, follow this process. Preheat the oven to 180 degrees Celsius for 20 minutes. Chop a medium-sized pumpkin in two halves, without peeling. Place them upside down in a roasting tin or a baking tray. Place the tray in the oven and bake for 60 minutes. The baking time varies from pumpkin to pumpkin, sometimes it may take 90 minutes or 45 minutes.

2. To check if the pumpkin is tender, prick it with the back of a spoon. If the spoon can pierce through, it is ready. Take the roasting tin out of the oven and place it on a cooling rack and allow it to cool completely. Then, use a spoon to scoop out the flesh put into a blender jar and pulse into a smooth puree. Set aside until required.

1 tsp vanilla extract
Zest of 1 orange
60 gm dried fig, chopped
¼ cup walnuts, chopped

For the cashew nut frosting
100 gm cashew nuts
60 ml coconut cream
4 tbsp honey
1 tsp vanilla extract
2 tbsp crushed walnuts, to decorate

3. Preheat the oven to 180 degrees Celsius. Grease an 8x4x3-inch loaf tin with butter and line the base with baking parchment.

4. In a bowl, add the eggs and sugar, and using a handheld whisk, whisk till smooth. Fold in all the other ingredients including the pumpkin puree. Tip the batter into the tin and bake for 50 minutes, or till a skewer inserted in the middle comes out clean.

5. Place the loaf tin on a cooling rack and let it cool in the tin for 15 minutes. Then, to unmould it, place a plate on top of the loaf tin and gently flip it. Tap the bottom of the loaf tin all over with your fingers to ensure even loosening of the cake.

6. To make the frosting, soak the cashew nuts in water for 20 minutes. Drain and add to a blender jar along with all the other ingredients apart from the crushed walnuts. Pulse until smooth.

7. As soon as cake has cooled completely, spread the frosting on top of the cake and decorate with crushed walnuts.

Banana-Walnut Loaf

To me, no matter how I'm feeling, the idea of cinnamon, banana and walnuts baked together in a cake is exciting enough to get into the kitchen and make this moist delight. This is a cake I love serving my guests on any day at teatime.

Using oil instead of butter helps keep this cake immensely moist and adding buttermilk enhances its crumbliness.

Prep time: 20 minutes | Baking time: 30–35 minutes | Serves: 6

Ingredients

250 gm extra ripe bananas, peeled
150 ml sunflower oil
(or any neutral oil)
250 gm caster sugar
2 large eggs
50 ml buttermilk
1½ tsp vanilla extract
½ cup walnuts, chopped
250 gm all-purpose flour
1 tsp cinnamon
2 tsp baking powder
½ tsp bicarbonate of soda

Method

1. Preheat the oven to 180 degrees Celsius. Grease an 8x4x3-inch loaf tin with butter and line with baking parchment. You can also use a 23-cm round cake tin.

2. Put the bananas in a large bowl and mash them using a fork. Now, add the oil, sugar, eggs, buttermilk and vanilla extract. Whisk till everything comes together. Stir in the walnuts.

3. Sift in the flour, cinnamon, baking powder and bicarbonate of soda. Gently fold in everything together. Tip the batter into the prepared tin and bake for 30–35 minutes, or till a skewer inserted in the centre comes out clean.

4. Place the loaf tin on a cooling rack and let it cool in the tin for 15 minutes. Then, to unmould it, place a plate on top of the loaf tin and gently flip it. Tap the bottom of the loaf tin all over with your fingers to ensure even loosening of the cake.

5. Allow it to rest for 10 more minutes and then slice and serve.

Almond and Chocolate Chip Muffins with Cashew Nut Frosting

One thing is for sure – people who are concerned about managing their weight are also the people who love to eat and dread having to miss out on any delicious food. Whenever I gain weight, I do so on account of eating lots of cakes, muffins, cupcakes, puddings and masala dosas. I can live without anything, but not without these food items. But the good news is that with this no-flour-no-butter muffin recipe I don't have to miss out on something I love so passionately. On the contrary, trying such new recipes and experiencing new flavours makes losing weight an exciting journey for me.

Almond flour is gluten-free, and it comes with its own nutty flavours. Flaxseeds are famous for their nourishing essential oils, and they not only keep the skin and hair healthy but also boost digestive health. Maple syrup with its caramelly sweetness is sugar in its most natural form. These muffins are not only cute to look at but are also packed with big flavours and healthy to eat.

There might be a few cracks on top, given the low fat content, just embrace them and ice them with my cashew nut frosting.

Prep time: 10 minutes | Baking time: 20–25 minutes | Makes: 12

Ingredients

For the cake

250 gm almond flour
65 gm ground flaxseeds
½ tsp bicarbonate of soda
2 tsp baking powder

Method

1. Preheat the oven to 180 degrees Celsius. Line a baking tray with muffin cases.

2. Add the flaxseeds to a blender jar and pulse them into a fine powder. Set aside until required.

3. To make the cake, add the almond flour, flaxseeds, bicarbonate of soda, baking powder, chocolate chips and chopped walnuts to a large mixing bowl.

50 gm chocolate chips
50 gm walnuts, chopped
65 gm yogurt
3 large eggs
100 ml maple syrup
50 ml sunflower oil
(or any neutral oil)
2 tsp almond essence

For the cashew nut frosting
100 gm cashew
50 ml coconut cream
4 tbsp honey
Juice of ½ lemon
1 tsp vanilla extract
2 tbsp chopped walnuts,
to decorate

4. In a jug, add the yogurt, eggs, maple syrup, oil and almond essence. Using a handheld electric whisk, blend all the ingredients till they are well combined.

5. Pour in the wet ingredients into the dry ingredients gradually to form a smooth batter. Use an ice cream scoop, or two spoons, fill the batter into the muffin cases. Bake for 20–25 minutes. Then, bring the tray out of the oven and place it on a cooling rack. Allow the muffins to cool inside the tray for 10 minutes, then take the muffins out of the muffin tray and place them on the cooling rack and allow them to cool completely.

6. In the meanwhile, make the frosting by adding all the ingredients for the frosting to a blender jar and pulsing them into a smooth paste. Spread it on top of the muffins and sprinkle some chopped walnuts.

Tutti-Frutti Cake

As a child, we usually spent summer vacations at my Nani's (maternal grandmother's) home. One of my brightest memories from those days is Nana (my maternal grandfather) taking me along with him on his morning walks. It was the most beautiful time – the air still had the night's coolness, the birds indulged in their early morning gossip, the trees felt greener than they feel at any other time of the day – everything felt harmonious and peaceful. On our way back, we'd often stop at a bakery and Nana would buy me my favourite cake: tutti-frutti cake. It was a light crumbly sponge studded with chewy, shiny dried fruits. It appeared similar to the stuff that I'd always imagined princesses from the fairy tales in my story book would eat. Did Cinderella or Princess Jasmine eat tutti-frutti cake? Perhaps not, but it felt exotic and helped satiate my fantasy of living in a castle full of sweet treats, teddy bears and every imaginable comfort.

This recipe comes from that same small bakery called Prem Bakery in my hometown of Shahdol in Madhya Pradesh. I got it from the owner's daughter Prachi, who was a batchmate in school. Many years after high school, we ran into each other enjoying kathi rolls at the same café in Bhopal. There was no end to that lovely evening, and this fruit cake and its recipe did come up between various other conversations.

If you find the sweetness of tutti-frutti a bit overwhelming, replace it with a combination of raisins, dried cranberries and dried apricots or with some natural-coloured glace cherries.

Prep time: 15 minutes | Baking time: 20 minutes | Serves: 8–10

Ingredients

250 gm + 1 tbsp all-purpose flour
200 gm tutti-frutti
225 gm butter
1 400-ml tin condensed milk

Method

1. Preheat the oven to 180 degrees Celsius. Grease and line an 8x4x3-inch loaf tin with baking parchment. You can also use 23-cm, round cake tin.

2. In a small bowl, add 1 tbsp of flour and the tutti-frutti and mix to coat well. This will prevent the tutti-frutti from sinking to the bottom and getting burnt during baking. Set aside.

4 large eggs
50 ml full-fat milk
2 tsp almond essence
1½ tsp baking powder

3. In a large bowl, whisk the butter and condensed milk until light and fluffy. Whisk in eggs, one by one, and then whisk in the milk and the almond essence.

4. In a separate bowl, sift together the flour and baking powder and then add the tutti-frutti. Mix everything well. Gently fold the dry ingredients into the wet ingredients.

5. Tip the batter into the loaf tin and bake for 18–20 minutes or until a skewer inserted into the centre comes out clean.

6. Place the loaf tin on a cooling rack and let it cool in the tin for 15 minutes. Then, to unmould it, place a plate on top of the loaf tin and gently flip it. Tap the bottom of the loaf tin all over with your fingers to ensure even loosening of the cake.

7. Allow it to rest for 10 minutes and then slice and serve.

Rosemary and Olive Focaccia

I often bake focaccia bread in anticipation of hectic mornings, because no matter how busy I am, I cannot leave my home without breakfast. It is also my go-to recipe while hosting guests at home, when I know I will not get to spend a lot of time in the kitchen. So, I bake a batch, wrap it in foil paper and store it in the refrigerator. When it's time for breakfast, I simply unwrap the foil and place the bread in a preheated oven. I wait for it to get just hot enough so the butter smeared on top melts completely. And there – without having to do much – I've got my early-morning breakfasts sorted out. The comforting, fulfilling nature of focaccia complements the uplifting flavour of a morning cup of English breakfast tea.

Prep time: 15 minutes | Cooking time: 20–25 minutes | Makes: 6–8

Ingredients

7 gm or 1 sachet of dry yeast
or 25 gm fresh yeast
1 tsp sugar
300 ml lukewarm water
500 gm all-purpose flour
50 ml olive oil + 2 tbsp + 2 tbsp
extra for drizzling
1/2 tsp salt
2 sprigs of rosemary
8–10 olives

Method

1. In a jug, add yeast, sugar and water. Use a fork to stir. Place it aside for yeast to dissolve.

2. In a large bowl, add flour, oil and salt. Use a spatula to mix everything. While stirring, gradually pour the liquid ingredients into the flour mix to form a loose dough. Turn the dough on the kneading surface (no need to sprinkle flour on the kneading surface) and knead it by pushing gently with your palm till it is smooth.

3. Now take out a medium-sized, rectangular tray. Drizzle 2 tbsp of olive oil and place the dough on the roasting tray. Use your fingers to flatten the dough so that it completely fits in the tray.

4. This will also create dimples on the dough.

5. Place the rosemary and olives into those dimples. Cover the tray with cling film or tea towel and keep it in a warm area for 40 minutes to prove.

6. Preheat the oven for 20 minutes at 220 degrees Celsius.

7. Once the dough is proven, drizzle 2 tbsp of olive oil, place the tray in the oven and bake for 20 minutes.

8. Take it out of the oven, place it on a cooling rack and allow it to cool for 15–20 minutes before serving.

Earl Grey

Curled up in an armchair while researching the development of the tea-drinking culture in England, I came across these beautiful lines written by Henry James. 'There are few hours in life more agreeable than the hour dedicated to the ceremony known as afternoon tea.'

The art of afternoon tea is a cherished art in England, and it all began with the seventh Duchess of Bedford, Anna Maria Russell. It is said that the duchess complained of hunger, or a sinking feeling, during the long gaps between lunch and dinner, and so she took some tea and a few things to eat to her private chambers. Later, she started inviting other ladies to take tea in her boudoir. By the mid-1850s, afternoon tea became an occasion for refined social contact, especially among women and became a more elaborate ritual. It was not long before all fashionable society was sipping tea with sandwiches and cakes between 3:30 and 5 p.m.

According to *The Ritz London Book of Afternoon Tea* by Helen Simpson, Earl Grey is an integral part of the ceremony of afternoon tea. I adore Earl Grey for its strong malty flavours imbued with the citrusy hint of Bergamot Orange. Pouches of Earl Grey tea have a much more permanent space in my purse than any make-up product. This is not because I doubt the hospitality of the places I am about to visit. It's just that I cannot just let my cup of tea rest upon chance. In addition, when I'm working or travelling for work, I am able to stay more focussed when I know that I can drink a nice cup of tea anytime I wish.

The book also says that afternoon tea must start with sandwiches and be followed by cake and scones. In my opinion, traditions, especially as precious as the art of afternoon tea must be followed just as they are, and these are my favourite sandwiches, cakes and scones to go with a hot cup of citrusy Earl Grey.

Achaari Chicken Cutlet Sandwich

(Pickled Chicken Cutlet Sandwich)

This sandwich packs a serious punch of flavours. Just imagine butter toasted bread slathered with pungent hot mayonnaise, topped with the crisp bites of chicken and the peppery crunch of lemon-soaked onion.

The oil from a jar of pickles in the mayonnaise sauce is what gives this sandwich its distinctive flavour and also its name. I often use the oil from the red chilli pickle my mother makes, but you can use whatever you have. I also suggest using panko breadcrumbs instead of regular ones as they add more crunch to the chicken. However, if they are not available, go with what you have. In fact, you can lightly toast some bread in the oven and then grind it down to make your own breadcrumbs. I recommend that you use good old-fashioned white bread for this sandwich and not the wholewheat.

Prep time: 15 minutes | Cooking time: 30 minutes | Serves: 4

Ingredients

4 boneless chicken thighs
2 tbsp yogurt
1 tsp red chilli powder
Salt, to taste
1 large onion, thinly sliced
1 large cucumber, thinly sliced
2 limes, juiced
1 cup all-purpose flour
2 eggs
1 cup breadcrumbs
Oil, for deep frying

Method

1. To marinate the chicken, put the chicken in a large bowl, add yogurt, red chilli powder and salt. Mix well, cover and put into the refrigerator for at least 2 hours. Take it out of the refrigerator at least 15 minutes before frying.

2. In a medium-sized bowl, add the onion and cucumber and then add the lime juice and salt to taste. Cover and set aside for as long as chicken is marinating.

3. To prepare your bread crumbing station, put the flour on a plate and season it with some salt. Crack the eggs in a bowl, add a pinch of salt and whisk. Put the breadcrumbs in another plate and season with a pinch of salt. Set aside until required.

White bread (or any bread of your choice)
1 tbsp dry garlic-and-coconut chutney (optional)

For the chilli pickle sauce
4 tbsp mayonnaise
1½ tbsp curd
1 tsp red chilli or mango pickle oil (you can also use mustard oil)
A pinch of red chilli powder
Juice of ½ lemon
1 tsp dill leaves, chopped
Salt, to taste

4. To make the chilli pickle sauce, add all the ingredients in a bowl and mix well. Set aside until required.

5. To fry the chicken, add oil to a deep pan and heat over a medium flame. Once it is hot, take the chicken out of the marination and first dredge in the flour. Dip the floured chicken in the egg mixture and then toss it in the breadcrumbs, ensuring that it is properly coated. Add the chicken to the oil, and fry over a medium flame till golden brown. Drain on absorbent paper and let it rest for 5 minutes.

6. To make the sandwiches, heat a pan over a medium flame, add some butter and toast the bread. Apply generous quantities of the chilli-pickle sauce on the toasted bread and arrange the fried chicken on one slice. Sprinkle garlic-coconut chutney over the chicken, top it with lemon-soaked onions and cucumbers and close the sandwich with another slice.

7. Cut the sandwich in half and enjoy.

Spicy Garlicky Paneer Sandwich

Paneer, most generously, lends itself to whatever flavours it is mixed with, but thankfully without losing its basic creaminess. It always feels as if the paneer in any dish is happy to socialize but refuses to be overpowered. Take this recipe for example – even when steeped in fiery hot chillies and pungent garlic, the paneer still maintains its gentle flavours. I guess this is what makes paneer such a great favourite across the country.

Just like many beautiful things in my life, the warm flavours of this sandwich are also a result of a happy coincidence. I once found all these ingredients in my refrigerator at the same time, demanding to be used. The spicy crunch of the vegetables punctuated by soft, comforting paneer makes this one a very cosy and safe sandwich. Please feel free to adjust the quantity of green chillies to your own taste but don't compromise on the flavours by using low-fat paneer.

Prep time: 30 minutes | Cooking time: 30 minutes | Serves: 4

Ingredients

1 clove of garlic
2–3 green chillies, finely chopped
1 tbsp oil
¼ cup fresh coriander, chopped
1 tsp cumin powder
Black salt, to taste
Juice of ½ lemon
1 cup paneer, cubed
½ cup sweet corn, steamed
½ cup capsicum, chopped
¼ cup onion, finely chopped
Slices of cheese
White bread (or any bread of your choice)
Butter

Method

1. Heat the oil in a pan, add cloves of garlic, sauté till brown speckles start to appear. Add green chilli and sauté till fragrant. Transfer to a blender jar, and add the coriander, cumin powder, black salt and lemon juice and blend to a smooth paste.

2. In a large bowl, put the paneer, corn, capsicum, onion and the garlic-chilli-coriander chutney, mix well. Taste and season if required.

3. Place a slice of bread on a chopping board, top it with the paneer mixture, place a slice of cheese on top and close it with another slice of bread. Press it gently together.

4. Heat a pan on medium heat. Apply butter generously to one side of the sandwich and sear it for 3–4 minutes in the pan. Flip the sandwich and apply butter on the other side and sear it for 3–4 minutes or till crisp and golden brown.

5. Cut in half and enjoy.

Victoria Sponge Cake

To me, this cake is something of a miracle because it is so truthfully itself with no extravagance of buttercream or any other fancy decorations. It has only a few basic ingredients, and it bakes into one of the best, most crumbly sponges ever. Personally, I'd rather have a Victoria sponge as my birthday cake over any other cake.

My favourite way to eat it is as a companion with my breakfast tea rather than with my evening tea because I prefer a robust cup of Assam tea in the morning, which loves the sweet, buttery flavours of the Victoria sponge whereas my evening cup of Darjeeling tea prefers flaky and crumbly flavours. You see, it is not me, it is the teas that have their own preferences.

Prep time: 15 minutes | Baking time: 25 minutes | Serves: 8

Ingredients

225 gm unsalted butter
225 gm sugar
4 eggs
1 tsp vanilla extract
225 gm all-purpose flour
A pinch of salt
1 tsp baking powder
1 tbsp milk

Method

1. Preheat the oven to 180 degrees Celsius. Prepare two 21-cm cake tins by greasing and lining them with baking parchment. Sift the flour and baking powder together.

2. In a mixing bowl, using a hand-held whisk or an electric blender, beat the butter till smooth, shiny and fluffy. Add sugar and beat till smooth. Add the eggs one by one and keep beating till fully incorporated. Add the vanilla extract. Fold in the flour, salt and baking powder gently. Add the milk and mix it in gently. Divide the batter between both cake tins equally.

3. Bake at 180 degrees Celsius for 25 minutes. Insert a skewer in the centre of the cake and remove if it comes out clean. Let the cakes cool inside the baking tin for 15 minutes. Then, invert over a cooling rack to cool completely.

For the filling
300 ml regular fresh cream
200 gm fruit jam

4. Place the cream in a bowl and beat with an electric hand blender until peaks form. Spread the cream on one of the sponges and jam on another and sandwich or join them together. Dust the top with icing sugar and enjoy with a hot cup of Earl Grey.

Scones

I firmly believe that an afternoon tea menu must have scones in it and over the past few years, I have tried many recipes for scones as Kunal, my England-returned husband, loves them, and has a great nostalgia for them. This recipe which I recently got from my neighbour Lynn, who happens to be from Manchester is the best so far. These scones are buttery, crumbly and mildly sweet – everything you imagine a scone to be.

Prep time: 20 minutes | Baking time: 20 minutes | Makes: 10–12

Ingredients
100 ml buttermilk
1 large egg
2 tsp vanilla extract
450 gm all-purpose flour
3 tsp baking powder
1 tsp bicarbonate of soda
100 gm sugar
120 gm salted butter, chilled
50 gm raisins
¼ tsp cinnamon powder

Method

1. Preheat the oven to 180 degrees Celsius. Line a flat baking tray, like a cookie tray, with baking parchment.

2. In a jug, add buttermilk, egg and vanilla and whisk everything together with the help of a fork. Set aside.

3. In a large mixing bowl, add the flour, baking powder, bicarbonate of soda, sugar, butter, raisins, and cinnamon powder. Use your fingers to mix everything together. We are looking for a breadcrumb consistency to the flour. Gently pour the wet mixture into the dry ingredients to form a soft dough. We are looking for everything to come together rather than get a smooth dough.

4. Now, sprinkle some flour on your work surface and place the dough on top. Flatten it slightly using your fingers, and with the help of rolling pin, roll the dough to 3-cm thickness. Using a small or large cookie cutter, cut out the scones and transfer them on to the baking tray.

For the glaze
1 egg yolk
4 tbsp milk

For the filling
100 ml double cream
Raspberry jam (or any other fruit jam of your choice)

5. To make the glaze, in a small bowl, add the egg yolk and milk and whisk using a fork. Use a pastry brush to brush this glaze on top of the scones and then bake for 15–20 minutes. As soon as they are out of oven, place the tray on a cooling rack and cool completely.

6. To make the filling, add the double cream to a mixing bowl and whisk to soft peaks using an electric hand blender.

7. Once the scones have cooled, cut them in half, spread jam on one half, cream on another half and join them together. Enjoy with a cup of Earl Grey.

Avocado Mash on Toast

The velvety nuttiness of avocado punctuated by the peppery crunch of spring onions, the sharp tang of lime juice and the refreshing earthiness of coriander leaves, spread thickly on a toasted bread paired with soothing Earl Grey is my idea of a heavenly breakfast on the go.

Prep time: 5 minutes | Cooking time: 5 minutes | Makes: 2

Ingredients

2 avocados
4 slices of bread (preferably sour dough)
2 spring onions, chopped
Juice of 1 lime
1 tbsp of coriander, chopped
1 tsp green chilli, chopped (optional)
2 tsp of olive oil
Black salt, to taste

Method

1. Lightly toast the slices of bread and keep aside to cool down.
2. Peel the avocado and scoop out the flesh in a bowl.
3. Add spring onions, lime juice, coriander, green chilli, olive oil and black salt. Mix well.
4. Spread it evenly on the toasted bread and enjoy.

Bagels

Making your own bagels can be something of a chore, definitely on a weekday. Yet, there are some moments during the weekends when you want to be anchored in the quiet of your kitchen and completely engrossed in kneading and folding, giving your mind a much-deserved break from the workaday world. Making your own batch of bagels is reserved for those times. This deeply calming activity will leave you with a smile on your face and a bagel in your hand. Gather around with your family and enjoy the freshly baked bagels with a thick layer of cream cheese smeared on top.

Prep time: 30 minutes | Cooking time: 15–20 minutes | Makes: 15

Ingredients

1 kg all-purpose flour
7 gm dried yeast or 25 gm fresh yeast
2 tsp salt
2 tbsp + 2 tbsp sugar
2 tbsp oil
500 ml tepid water
2 tbsp sesame seeds, to sprinkle

Method

1. Line a large roasting tin with baking parchment.
2. In a large mixing bowl, add flour, yeast, salt, 2 tbsp of sugar and oil. Mix well.
3. Gradually pour in the tepid water a little at a time and knead till the dough becomes hard.
4. Place the dough in a well-oiled bowl, cover it with cling film and place it in a warm place to prove for one hour.
5. After that turn the dough on a kneading surface sprinkled with flour. Knead it again into a smooth ball. Now, use your palm to roll the dough from the large side into a cylindrical shape and cut it into 15 pieces.

6. Roll each piece into a thin cylindrical shape, and join the two ends to make a circle. Repeat with every piece. Place the pieces on the baking sheet, cover with a tea towel and allow them to prove for 20 minutes.

7. Simultaneously, preheat the oven to 220 degrees Celsius.

8. Bring water to a boil in a large pan and add sugar. Drop in the bagels. Boil them for a minute on each side and take them out using a spatula. Place the bagels on a baking sheet and sprinkle some sesame seeds on top. Put the tray in the oven and bake for 20 minutes.

9. Once you take them out of the oven, place them on a cooling rack for 15 minutes before serving them.

Darjeeling

The British, as happy as they were to find tea in Assam, still craved the floral notes of Chinese black tea. As soon as they had their first batch of tea processed with the help of the Singphos in Assam, they managed to smuggle some *Camellia sinensis var. sinensis* plants and a few tea artists out of China. At first, those plants were planted in the tea-growing regions of Assam, but the plants could not survive the heat of Assam's lowland climate. Hence, they were removed from Assam and were planted in the botanical gardens in the foothills of Himalayas.

Meanwhile, Darjeeling was being developed as a summer retreat for the British soldiers posted in Kolkata, just as Ooty was for soldiers in Chennai and Mussoorie was for soldiers in Delhi. The hill station was discovered by two British soldiers named Captain George Lloyd and J.W. Grant, who were deployed by the British government to resolve a geo-political issue between Sikkim and Nepal. As Jeff Koehler tells us in his book *Darjeeling: A History of the World's Greatest Tea*, on their way Lloyd and Grant stopped at an 'old Gorkha station called Dorjeling.' They were awestruck by its beauty and cold climate, and they prepared a full report on Darjeeling's potential as a hill station retreat and submitted it to the government.

In those days, Darjeeling was under the jurisdiction of kingdom of Sikkim. Soon enough, after Lloyd and Grant submitted their report, the area was leased by the British government from the Raja of Sikkim. Thus, the process of Darjeeling becoming the brightest jewel in the global tea crown was initiated. According to the books *The History of the Indian Tea Industry* by Sir Percival Griffiths and Jeff Koehler's *Darjeeling: A History of the World's Greatest Tea*, the credit for developing Darjeeling into a beautiful hill station and planting the first tea bushes goes to Dr Campbell of the Indian Medical Service who was posted as the superintendent of the new territory in 1839. Under his tenure, the process of turning this dense forest into a beautiful hill station was rapid and remarkable.

According to Jeff Koehler, in 1841, just two years after arriving, Campbell planted tea in the gardens of his own residence, known as Beachwood, with the plants that came from the nurseries in the Himalayan foothills. In 1853, Campbell stated in a report that some two thousand tea plants, ranging from 12-year-old bushes to seedlings of a few months were growing at elevations ranging from 2,000 to 7,000 feet. With governmental backing, Campbell established tea nurseries in Darjeeling and Kurseong with both Assam and China leaves. By

With Rajah Banerjee, the fourth-generation owner of Makaibari Tea Estate.

1856, it was reported that tea plants had been sown and raised in Tukvar, Kurseong, Canning and Hopetown. More gardens quickly followed including Makaibari, Pandam, Ging, Ambootia, Takdah and Phoobsering. The first tea factory in Darjeeling opened in Makaibari in 1859, and by 1874, Darjeeling had 113 tea gardens with a production of 1.78 million kilograms. Today, Darjeeling has 87 tea gardens with more than 17,500 hectares of land under tea cultivation, producing more than ten million kilograms of tea every year.

My first stop on my way to Darjeeling Hill was Siliguri. I was there to meet Rajah Banerjee, the fourth-generation owner of the Makaibari Tea Estate, and one of the most famous personalities in the Indian tea world. His great-grandfather Girish Chandra Banerjee was a pioneer Indian tea planter and had worked alongside Dr Campbell. The story of Rajah taking up the leadership is a very interesting one – it seems more like a cosmic plan. Young Rajah was studying to become a mechanical engineer at the Imperial College in London. When he came back home for a holiday after four years, his father bought him a gun to hunt with, and while he was on a hunting expedition, his horse was struck by a wild boar and the panicked horse threw Rajah off his back. It was that moment which changed his fate.

According to the famous story, which Rajah has also mentioned in full detail in his book *Rajah of Darjeeling Organic Tea*, 'In the split second that I fell, I perceived a brilliant band of white light, connecting me to the trees in the forest around me, the woods sang out melancholy in an incredible concerto, "Save us! Save us!"' After this experience Rajah decided to stay back in India and dedicate his life to tea.

He proposed organic farming to his father, but his father vehemently opposed it as organic farming methods implied a lower yield. But Rajah was not ready to let go, and so with the help of a few tea makers, he worked in secret and practised organic tea farming on a small patch inside Makaibari. He was able to get that tea processed separately, and his father praised the flavours. Rajah had managed to keep his harvest secret for a whole year before finally revealing his organic undertaking. Pleasantly surprised by the new and more refreshing flavours, his father supported Rajah's ideas of organic farming and they were implemented across the estate.

Everyone was taught composting techniques, and the estate began to transform into a holistic harmonious tea farm that did not use chemicals. His book comes with the DVD of a documentary made on Makaibari, in which he mentions his struggle to establish organic practices. 'All my neighbours thought I was a sort of witch, doing witchcraft with tea, and stayed away from it, from the crazy man. It was only after Makaibari teas started making a great name and money in the international market that every garden started to practise the organic farming. I was astonishingly propelled from laughing stock to pioneer,' Rajah wrote in his book. Today, according to the Darjeeling Tea Association, 77 of Darjeeling's 87 estates are organic.

The next day, I had travelled from Siliguri to Kurseong to tour the terrains of the Makaibari Tea Estate, and it was thrilling to be there. I enjoyed talking to tea makers there, and they explained what went into making such a distinctive tea. Each worker was fully devoted to tea, and from what I gathered, the most important factor behind a successful batch of tea is the human connection. There is no written formula or a recipe, just like my mother's cooking, it is solely based on experience and instincts.

Sanjay Das, the manager at Makaibari tea estate also gave me an insight into what makes Darjeeling so special. He said, 'Darjeeling is blessed with a topography, or the arrangement of natural physical features, most suitable for the growth of tea bushes. The sunshine is perfect, neither too harsh nor too mild. It never rains less than 140 inches, plus the steep slant structure of the hills provides excellent natural drainage which saves it from swamping, and the beautiful mountain mists helps the tea leaves stay moisturized, but most importantly the cold air from the Himalayas keeps a check on humidity and that's what makes the Darjeeling's flavours so crisp.'

After Makaibari, I continued my journey to cross the Teesta River to reach the Glenburn Tea Estate. It was not easy to traverse the dirt track, but I am glad I let my inner tea nerd lead the way or I would have never known the panoramic beauty of Glenburn Tea Estate – a lush, green valley, dotted with vintage bungalows with vines of orange trumpets hanging from entrance arches, a beautiful pomelo tree, manicured lawns, antique hand-carved wooden furniture, shiny cutlery, precious tea sets, and most of all, an uninterrupted view of Kanchenjunga.

On my first day, the view of Kanchenjunga was covered by clouds, and this was making me sad. Guessing my feelings, Bertie, the manager of the resort, most dramatically remarked 'You'll see it if Kanchenjunga wishes to be seen.' I prayed to Kanchenjunga and on the second day, my wish was granted. Bright sunshine filled my room as I opened the windows, and the clouds cleared up to show me the majestic beauty of world's third-tallest peak. True to its name, five shimmering white peaks covered the sky. There's a very popular belief among locals, which enhances the beauty of Kanchenjunga for me: it is said that the breath of God blows cool air over the hills of Darjeeling from these mountains and brings mist, fog and moisture that nurtures the neat rows of the tea bushes that follow the steep contours of the valleys. This is the reason behind the unique flavour of Darjeeling tea.

'The Glenburn Tea Estate stretches from a height of 1,000 feet to 3,500 feet, and with such a range, the estate contains a number of microclimates, which is also true of each tea estate in Darjeeling,' explained Mahesh Lama, a young passionate, second-generation tea maker and manager of Glenburn. By microclimate, Mahesh means that depending upon their position from the sun, within each garden lies a different climate zone: tropical, temperate or alpine. The lower areas of a garden catch more sun and have higher humidity, resulting in tropical climatic conditions, which makes the leaves grow faster with slightly stronger flavours. The temperate, relatively colder climate of the mid-sections have lower yields but delicate flavours. In the alpine cold of the upper reaches, the tea leaf takes its own time to unfurl, this unhasty growth results in more pronounced floral flavours imbued with a hint of fruity sweetness but with a very low yield.

'Only the right leaves can make the right tea,' said Hrishikesh Lama, the factory manager, as we started our factory tour in the withering room. 'Plucking is a work of patience mixed with skill, and that's why pluckers are always women. Their nimble fingers always select and pick without spoiling the two leaves and bud, or what we call dwi pat suiro in Nepali, which are softer, newer and brighter,' he finished. After being plucked, these delicate leaves are withered, rolled, oxidized, and then dried. The thing to observe here is that unlike Assam or Munnar, all of Darjeeling tea is Orthodox tea and leaves are left whole rather than being processed by the CTC method.

Once dried, the leaves are sorted in four categories: whole leaf, broken leaf, fanning and dust. Whole leaf teas are further categorized based on size of the processed leaf, and bigger the leaf, the better. The highest level is FTGFOP, which stands for Finest Tippy Golden Flowery Orange Pekoe, although these teas end up becoming so expensive that tea industry folks often joke that the acronym really stands for 'far too good for ordinary people.'

After Glenburn, I went further up the hill to reach Darjeeling. My journey from the foot of the hill (Siliguri) to its top (Darjeeling) made me truly experience what Rajah Banerjee said: 'These sharp variations in altitude makes you travel across three major climate zones – the tropical, temperate and Alpine cold – within three to four hours. This is not possible anywhere else in the world in a such small biotope, giving rise to the vast diversity of flora and fauna in the region, and tea is only a bonus from this enormous diversity.'

In Darjeeling, I was set to meet Bhuvan Sarda of Nathmulls Tea. The Sardas have been selling their teas in Darjeeling for more than 90 years now, and it was Bhuvan's grandfather Nathmull Sarda who established the shop, with two more in the town now. Sitting by the window in the tea lounge inside his shop, overlooking a beautiful view of snowy mountains with narrow tops and a deep valley on both sides while sipping on some Darjeeling tea we started our conversation by discussing the concept of flush because it doesn't merely convey the season in which the tea leaves are harvested and processed, but also conveys the flavours and aroma to expect from the tea.

In the words of Bhuvan Nathmull, 'As you would have seen, every tea is labelled with information about which flush it belongs to, which garden it comes from, and what its leaf grade is. So, one of the most common questions is which is the best flush? Honestly, there's no answer to that question – it depends on the time of the day actually. In the morning, I prefer a strong cup of Darjeeling, which I get from second flush tea, better known as Muscatel – it's a beautiful combination of flavours which could be smoky, malty, smooth, and yet carry a fruity note. As the day progresses, I prefer a light-bodied Darjeeling, which most likely will be a first flush tea. They are bit grassy and astringent but if you take the time to appreciate it, you will realize that it's flowery as well and its sweet aftertaste lingers in your mouth for a very long time.'

Darjeeling holds the same place in the world of tea that champagne does in the world of

At Nathmulls, the oldest retailers of tea in Darjeeling.

wine or truffles in the world of mushrooms. In every season or the flush, it is one of the most sought-after tea, and in the words of Vikram Mittal, a tea taster, blender and a trader in New Delhi for more than 30 years, 'It's a complex flavour, not easy to describe in words but can be called fruity, like peaches. It has floral notes as well, with a long-lasting sweet aftertaste.'

Let me now explain the concept of flushes as I understand them and share my favourite recipes to go along with them. I hope it helps you to select the most suitable flush for yourself.

First Flush or Spring Tea (February–April)

Teas produced from February till late April are known as first flush teas, and they mark the start of a new season for a tea bush. In the hills of Darjeeling, tea bushes 'sleep' for the cold months from November, December and January. The season starts with mild spring rains in late January, gently kissing the tea bushes into wakefulness. There's still a mild nip in the air, short rains and the mild spring sun makes everything fresh with their soft gentle touch, and this phenomenon is not just confined to the tea gardens. Lots of fresh vegetation sprouts up all over the hills. It is this harmony and happiness in nature that gets carried into the cup in first flush teas, renowned all over the world as spring teas. They usually have delicate floral notes with a gentle fruitiness and a hint of a citrusy herbal tone.

Glenburn's Apple, Walnut and Cinnamon Cake

The ethnic mix in Darjeeling is very diverse: the Gorkhas, Lepchas, Tibetans, Bhutanese, Burmese, Marwadis and Bengalis have all come together in Darjeeling, bringing their languages, entertainment and cuisines with them. During my six-day trip, I tasted multiple versions of the legendary Burmese lahpet thoke (fermented tea leaf salad), a variety of spicy, silky noodles and flavourful Tibetan dumplings and stews. But it was the luxurious cakes and cookies at the Glenburn Tea Estate, I had with my tea through the day that I wanted to bring home to my own kitchen.

As heavenly as Glenburn itself, bestowed with fullness like that corner of the earth, and served under a pomelo tree, each bite of this cake was magical. I was determined not to leave the place without the recipe, and the chefs at Glenburn were generous and kind enough to share it.

The fresh, subtle sweet notes of apples, the crunch of walnuts and the comfort of cinnamon creates a cheerful rhythm of flavours that makes you want to take a bite of this cake, sip your tea, then take a bite, then again a sip of your tea in an unending loop till you are ready for a refill.

Prep time: 30 minutes | Baking time: 60–90 minutes | Serves: 8–10

Ingredients

450 gm red apples, peeled and chopped
Juice of 1 lemon
2 tbsp sugar
1 tsp cinnamon powder

Method

1. Preheat the oven to 180 degrees Celsius, and grease and line a 23-cm round cake tin with baking parchment.

2. Heat a pan, add the chopped apples, lemon juice, sugar and the cinnamon powder. Cook gently over a low flame for 10–12 minutes. Take off the heat and allow to cool.

225 gm salted butter
225 gm brown sugar
4 large eggs
225 gm all-purpose flour
2 tsp baking powder
A pinch of salt
100 gm walnuts, chopped
1 tsp vanilla extract

3. In separate bowl, add butter and brown sugar, using a handheld whisk or an electric whisk, whisk till they become smooth. Whisk in the eggs one by one. Sift in the flour, salt and baking powder. Add the walnuts and vanilla extract. Gently fold everything in.

4. Spoon half of the cake batter in the prepared tin and then spread a layer of the prepared apple mixture. Spoon the remaining batter on top. Level the surface of the cake with an offset spatula, and then sprinkle some brown sugar and walnuts.

5. Bake for 1–1½ hours, ensuring you check after one hour, or until properly risen and golden brown on top. Leave to cool in the tin for a minimum of 15 minutes and then turn out onto a cooling rack. Cool for 15 minutes. Place the cake on a chopping board, a serving plate or a cake stand and dust with icing sugar. Cut and serve.

Rose and Cardamom Cake

With the luxurious notes of cardamom transitioning into the woody smokiness of rose, this cake is my idea of nirvana. It's not exactly the right thing to play favourites, but this cake is my most favourite teatime delight.

Prep time: 20 minutes | Baking time: 35–40 minutes| Serves: 8–10

Ingredients

2 tsp rose water
A pinch of saffron
225 ml yogurt
225 gm salted butter
225 gm caster sugar
4 large eggs
350 gm all-purpose flour
¼ tsp bicarbonate of soda
1½ tsp baking powder
2 tsp cardamom powder
50 gm pistachios, chopped

For the glaze (optional)

100 gm white chocolate
2 tbsp milk

Method

1. Preheat the oven to 180 degrees Celsius. Grease a 23-cm round cake tin with high sides, and line it with baking parchment.

2. Add the saffron and rose water to the yogurt and set aside.

3. In a separate bowl, add the butter and sugar, and using a handheld or an electric whisk, whisk till they become smooth. Whisk in the eggs one by one. As soon as the eggs are incorporated, whisk in the rose water, yogurt and saffron mixture. Whisk till everything is smooth. Sift in the flour, bicarbonate of soda and baking powder. Add the cardamom powder and pistachios and gently fold everything in.

4. Tip the batter into the baking tin and bake to 180 degrees Celsius for 35–40 minutes, or until a skewer inserted into the centre comes out clean. Allow the cake to cool in the tin for 10 minutes and then transfer to a cooling rack. Let it cool for 15 more minutes, then peel off the baking parchment. Place it on a chopping board, a serving plate or a cake stand. Allow it to stand while you prepare the glaze.

5. To make the glaze, place the white chocolate in a saucepan along with the milk. Simmer gently on low heat till the chocolate is melted. Cool for 5–6 minutes and then drizzle on top of the cake. Ensure the cake is completely cooled before you drizzle the glaze.

Windamere's Blueberry Crumble Muffins

Situated at the top of Observatory Hill in Darjeeling, Windamere was a cosy boarding house during colonial times, a home away from home for bachelor British tea traders. It has now been transformed into a heritage hotel, and its Victorian cottages would easily inspire nostalgia in the heart of any English traveller. Stay packages at Windamere include full meal plans, and your day starts on the delicious note of a slow-cooked porridge and a cheese and onion pie.

Come the afternoon and the fireplaces in the Windamere's renowned Daisy's Music Room light up to celebrate the British art of afternoon tea. A lady wearing a lacy, white apron serves tea from carved silver teapots followed by generous helpings of crisp biscuits, light scones smothered with jam and clotted cream, cool cucumber sandwiches, fruit tea cakes and blueberry crumble muffins.

Everything was elegantly delicious, but it was the muffins that inspired me most – crumbly with a subtly sweet, light-as-air sponge studded with oozing purplish blueberries. I just could not stop thinking about them on my way home. As they say, seek and ye shall find, and indeed, I sought out the recipe and the good people of Windamere shared it with me.

Prep time: 30 minutes | Baking time: 25–30 minutes |
Makes: 6 jumbo muffins or 12 regular ones

Ingredients

70 gm salted butter
170 gm caster sugar
1 egg
270 gm all-purpose flour
2½ tsp baking powder
190 ml full-fat milk
Juice of 1 lemon

Method

1. Preheat the oven to 180 degrees Celsius and line a muffin tray with paper cases.

2. To make the crumble, in a bowl, place the flour, cold butter and sugar, and rub them with the tip of your fingers till they resemble breadcrumbs. Store in the refrigerator until required.

1 tsp vanilla extract
100 gm fresh blueberries, reserving a few for garnish

For the crumble
75 gm all-purpose flour
25 gm caster sugar
50 gm cold butter

3. To make the muffins, in a large bowl, place the butter and sugar and whisk them till they are light and fluffy. Whisk in the egg and combine well. Sift in the flour and baking powder and then gently fold them in. Gradually whisk in the milk and lemon juice. Fold in the vanilla extract and blueberries.

4. Spoon in the mixture into the muffin cases until they are three-fourths full. Generously cover with crumble to form a small dome over the batter and then dot with blueberries. Bake at 180 degrees Celsius for 25–30 minutes or until a skewer comes out clean.

5. Rest the muffins in the tray for 5 minutes and then unmould them. Let them cool for 15 minutes before serving.

Darjeeling Second Flush or Muscatel Tea (May–June)

The unique combination of the climatic factors, rains, heat and humidity during the summer in the mountains of Darjeeling completely changes the flavour profiles of the tea. It acquires much more of a fruity note and loses the slight astringency which is present in the first flush.

Second flush teas carry an elegant apricot sweetness in their flavour. The heat also induces nutty notes of caramel and a deep amber colour. The flavours of the second flush starkly resemble the flavour of a wine called Muscatel, and this tea is also known by the name Muscatel Flush among tea enthusiasts.

Angel Almond Cake

With a gleaming golden crown of toasted almonds adorning a sweet, nutty, vanilla sponge, this cake was surely meant for fairies. The second flush is a divine flavour, even a slight contrast can ruin it. The best way to find its perfect match in food is by trying to mirror its flavours and that is what this cake is all about – pairing delicate flavours.

Prep time: 20 minutes | Baking time: 45 minutes | Serves: 6–8

Ingredients

3 large eggs
120 gm caster sugar
½ cup full-fat milk
2 tsp vanilla extract
75 gm unsalted butter, melted and cooled
150 gm all-purpose flour
1½ tsp baking powder
65 gm ground almonds (or almond meal)

For the topping

100 gm unsalted butter
75 gm brown sugar
50 ml full-fat milk
150 gm almonds, flaked

Method

1. Preheat the oven to 180 degrees Celsius. Grease and line a 23-cm round baking tin with baking parchment.

2. To make the sponge, in a large bowl, place the eggs and sugar and whisk them till they are fluffy. Whisk in the milk, vanilla extract and melted butter. Sift in the flour and baking powder. Fold in the ground almonds. As soon as the batter is smooth, transfer it to the cake tin and bake at 180 degrees Celsius for 30–35 minutes.

3. Start preparing the topping 10 minutes before taking the cake out of the oven. Place the butter in a saucepan over a medium flame. After it has melted, add the brown sugar and milk, bring it to a boil and add the almonds. Let it bubble for 1 minute.

4. After the cake is baked for 30–35 minutes, take it out of the oven carefully. With the help of a spoon or a spatula, spread the caramel mixture evenly on top of the cake, put it back in the oven and bake for 10–15 minutes or till the topping is golden.

5. Remove from the oven and leave it to cool for 15 minutes inside the tin. Run a knife around the edge to loosen the cake. Unmould it from the tin and let it cool for 30 minutes.

6. Slice with a sharp knife, serve and enjoy with tea.

Coconut Cake with Lemon Drizzle

Soothing sweetness of coconut generously drizzled with the refreshing tang of lemon, this cake and delicate flavours of Darjeeling tea are just meant to be.

Prep time: 15 minutes | Baking time: 35–40 minutes | Serves: 6–8 people

Ingredients

125 gm salted butter
125 gm sugar
4 large eggs
125 gm self-raising flour
100 gm desiccated coconut
2 tbsp milk

For the drizzle

200 gm icing sugar
Juice of 1 lemon

Method

1. Preheat the oven to 180 degrees Celsius. Grease and line an 18-cm loaf tin with baking parchment. You can also use mini loaf tins if you prefer.

2. In a bowl, beat butter and sugar till creamy. Add the eggs one by one until well combined. Sift in the flour and add the desiccated coconut and milk. Mix gently. Tip the batter into the cake tin. Bake at 180 degrees Celsius for 35–40 minutes or until an skewer inserted in the centre comes out clean. Let the cake cool completely.

3. To prepare the drizzle, add lemon juice to the icing sugar gradually while whisking constantly. Drizzle over your cake and top up with some mint leaves or lemon zest.

Amaretti

Consuming a countless number of these Italian almond biscuits at Glenburn was not only about their taste – it was also about my nostalgia for Italy. I loved my time in Italy both inside and outside culinary school, and the café that my friends and I hung out after school served these moon-shaped almond biscuits complimentary with their cappuccino. I enjoyed their sweet comforting chewiness laced with floral sweetness of almond very much, and I always wanted to come back and bake my own – it's lucky for me that they were part of my curriculum.

Now whenever I bake my own, I can't get enough of their crumbly texture covered with icing sugar in patches. For me, it somewhat echoes the view of the snow-capped peaks of the Kanchenjunga Mountain that I enjoyed while sitting in Glenburn.

Prep time: 30 minutes | Baking time: 10–12 minutes | Makes: 15–20

Ingredients

280 gm ground almonds (or almond meal)
120 gm caster sugar
1 tsp almond essence
3 egg whites
A pinch of salt
4–5 tbsp icing sugar

Method

1. Preheat the oven to 170 degrees Celsius. Line a baking tray with baking parchment.

2. In a bowl, place the ground almonds, sugar and almond essence and mix well.

3. In a separate bowl, add the egg whites and a pinch of salt. Using an electric hand blender, whisk till fluffy. Then, gently fold in the ground almonds, caster sugar and almond essence mixture into the egg whites. Cover the bowl with cling film and cool in the refrigerator for 30 minutes.

4. Spread the icing sugar on a plate. Take the mixture out of the refrigerator and using a tablespoon, scoop one measure in your hands and roll it into a smooth ball. Then, roll it in the icing sugar and place it on the baking tray. Use the same method to make the balls out of the whole mixture and place them a little apart from each other. Place the tray in the oven and bake at 170 degrees Celsius for 10–12 minutes.

5. Once done, take the tray out, place it on a cooling rack and let the biscuits cool in the tray for 15 minutes. Take the tray off the cooling rack and using a flat spatula, very gently, lift the amarettis and place them back on the cooling rack. Cool for at least 30 minutes.

6. Enjoy with a hot cup of tea.

Darjeeling Autumn Flush (October–November)

The autumn flush season is a short one, just like the short hours of sunlight during this time. The winter starts to set in, and things start to slow down a bit, including the growth in the tea leaves. This slow growth allows for plenty of time for the flavours to develop, resulting in a satisfying complexity in flavours. Autumn flush tea has dominant floral notes but a rather gentle approach. It seems more like a mix of zesty fruits and musky spices, similar to a Christmas pudding. A lower caffeine content makes these tea leaves more suitable for processing into an oolong or a white tea. I love autumn flush for its refreshing woody fragrance and deep burgundy liquor.

Carrot Cake Mini Loafs with Cream Cheese Frosting

The flavour of autumn flush is complex and has an affinity only for something equally complex. Keeping that in mind, I think that spiced fruit cakes are the best option as an accompaniment. With the gentle hint of aromatic spices knitted into the creamy comforts of carrots, this cake and the caramelly notes of autumn flush is a marriage made in heaven.

Prep time: 30 minutes | Baking time: 10–12 minutes | Makes: 15–20

Ingredients

175 gm all-purpose flour
½ tsp bicarbonate of soda
2 tsp baking powder
1 tsp cinnamon powder
1 tsp nutmeg powder
1 tsp mixed spice powder
½ tsp ground cloves
A pinch of salt
2 large eggs
200 gm caster sugar
200 ml sunflower oil
200 gm carrots, grated
75 gm walnuts, ground

Method

1. Preheat the oven to 150 degrees Celsius. Grease and line a 23-cm cake tin or several mini loaf tins with baking parchment.

2. Sift the flour, bicarbonate of soda, baking powder, cinnamon powder, nutmeg powder, mixed spice powder, ground cloves and salt together and set aside.

3. In a mixing bowl, place the egg, sugar and oil and beat well. Stir in the carrot and walnuts. Fold in the dry ingredients very gently with a rubber spatula. Don't whisk or stir or too much air will be incorporated, and you will get very dense carrot cake instead of a fluffy one. Pour the batter into the baking tray.

4. Bake at 150 degrees Celsius for an hour or quarter of an hour. To check if the cake is done, a skewer inserted into the centre of the cake should come out clean. If it doesn't, pop it back into the oven for 5–10 minutes.

For the orange cream cheese icing
250 gm cream cheese
50 gm butter
275 gm icing sugar
1 tsp vanilla essence
2 tsp orange essence or the zest of two oranges

5. Allow the cake to cool in the tin for 10 minutes and then transfer to a cooling rack. Cool for 15 more minutes and then peel off the baking parchment. Place it on a chopping board, serving plate or cake stand while you prepare the icing.

6. For the icing, place everything in a bowl and beat together till smooth. Once the cake is completely cooled, spread it on the cake using a spoon or you can pipe with a piping bag and your favourite nozzle. You can make just one cake or make two cakes and sandwich them together with cream cheese frosting. Garnish with chopped walnuts.

Lemon Lavender Cake

My heart always beats faster at the sight of neat rows of tea cakes and muffins in a café – I receive more gratification from staring at that sight than at any other art. This recipe was inspired by my favourite French café in Muscat called Paul. I love their lemon blueberry cake and can never get enough of it. The sharpness of lemon in a sweet sponge makes this one of my favourite cakes with tea.

This is a glistening golden sponge infused with the refreshing breath of lavender, wrapped around in snow-white frosting of royal icing and adorned with crown of blueberries sitting on top – it doesn't get prettier than this!

Prep time: 15 minutes | Baking time: 30–40 minutes | Makes: 6

Ingredients

80 gm salted butter
300 gm sugar
5 large eggs
140 ml fresh cream
1 tsp dried lavender flowers
Zest of 3 lemons or juice of 1 big lemon
240 gm all-purpose flour
2 tsp baking powder

For the glaze

20 ml lemon juice
100 gm icing sugar
Blueberries and mint for decoration

Method

1. Preheat the oven to 180 degrees Celsius. Grease and line an 8x4x3-inch loaf tin or properly grease a small bundt cake tin, ensure that every nook and corner is greased properly.

2. In a bowl, beat the butter and sugar together until creamy. Add the eggs one by one. Whisk in the cream, lavender flowers and lemon zest or juice.

3. In a separate bowl, sift in the flour and baking powder. Fold in the dry ingredients into wet ingredients until well combined.

4. Pour the batter in the cake tin and bake at 180 degrees Celsius for 30–40 minutes or until a skewer inserted in the centre comes out clean.

4. Allow the cake to cool in the tin for 10 minutes and then transfer to a cooling rack. Cool for 15 more minutes and then peel off the baking parchment. Place it on a chopping board, serving plate or cake stand while you prepare the icing.

5. To make the icing, place the icing sugar in a bowl and gradually add the lemon juice. You may not use all the juice as we are looking for a coating consistency icing, which forms a velvety lemony crust on the cake. Spread on the cake once it has completely cooled.

6. Top the glaze with blueberries and sprinkle mint leaves.

Oatmeal and Raisin Cookies

The knowledge that there is something resting in the refrigerator or filled in my snack jars to go with my morning cup of tea helps me sleep well. You see, no matter how much I love being in the kitchen, I love hassle-free mornings, full of sweet nothings and strong tea too. These cookies are my way of ensuring just that kind of morning.

Loaded with the goodness of oats and raisins, these cookies are moist and fudgy, pairing well with the enchantingly complex flavours of the Darjeeling autumn flush.

Prep time: 20 minutes | Baking time: 12 minutes | Makes: 18–20 cookies

Ingredients

170 gm butter
200 gm brown sugar
70 gm white sugar
3 large eggs
130 gm all-purpose flour
1 tsp cinnamon powder
¼ tsp bicarbonate of soda
2 tsp vanilla extract
200 gm instant oats
85 gm raisins

Method

1. Preheat the oven to 180 degrees Celsius. Line a cookie baking tray with parchment.

2. In a large mixing bowl, add butter and both the sugars, using an electric hand-held blender or a hand-held whisk, whisk till smooth. Whisk the eggs in one at a time. Add the flour, cinnamon and bicarbonate of soda, vanilla extract, oats and raisins and fold till everything comes together. This is a very loose dough.

3. Dip your hands in water briefly and place a tablespoon full of the dough between your palms and roll it into smooth ball. Place it on the baking tray. Once you are done forming cookies from the whole batter, gently tap them with your fingers to flatten them.

4. Bake in a preheated oven at 180 degrees Celsius for 12 minutes and then take the tray out. Rest the cookies on the tray for at least 15 minutes and use a spatula to transfer them onto a cooling rack. Cool for at least 30 minutes before serving.

This feels like
the start of
something
good

Alle Saang, the Foot-Rolled Tea of Arunachal Pradesh

As I took my first sip, I could not help but think the setting was more than a little unusual for me. I was not sitting comfortably in a lovely tea café but was standing in middle of a dense forest just outside Mirrem village in east Arunachal Pradesh, a region known for its strong culture of tea. Boke, a local tea artist, had just cut a segment of a bamboo from the bamboo grove, filled it with water from his bottle, taken out a pouch of tea leaves, added some to the water, built a fire from a pile of dead leaves on ground and made us some tea. 'Customarily, we never travel without carrying tea,' said Boke, while pouring this perfectly brewed tea into my bamboo mug.

My journey had begun in Pasighat, the oldest town in the Siang district of Arunachal Pradesh, home to one of the most celebrated tea estates in India, the Donyi Polo Tea Estate. They were recently in the news for their golden needle tea, which was sold at the record price for ₹75,000 per kilo, making it the most expensive white tea ever sold at any auction in India.

Before making my way towards Mirrem, I had made a stop at Donyi Polo for a day lured by its record-breaking teas. My day there was mostly spent in its tasting room sampling its wide variety of teas and touring the tea estate. It was a huge tea estate spread across the lower and upper Siang district. The area which falls in the lower part of the Siang district has a hot, humid climate suitable for malting, hence producing teas with rich, malty flavours. In contrast, the area in the eastern part of the Siang district, due to its proximity to Himalayan glaciers, has a colder, drier climate and produces teas with delicate floral flavours. Just like the twelfth-century Japanese monk Myõan Eisai wrote in his book *Kissa Yojoki: How to Stay Healthy by Drinking Tea*, 'Growing up in the mountains and valleys, it contains the very spirit of the earth.' With their tea that has rich, malty flavours, Donyi Polo produces CTC or the chai patti, and with their tea that has delicate floral flavours, they produce four varieties of speciality teas: black orthodox, white, green and oolong.

At Donyi Polo, Manoj, the manager of the tea estate, and his wife Leena invited me to dinner.

As we tucked into some barbecued chicken smothered with bhut jolokia (Bhutan pepper) chutney and dung po, which is Arunachali steamed rice cake, around a bonfire at Donyi Polo's beautiful guesthouse, we also chatted about tea, and Manoj explained their recent discovery, purple tea.

Purple tea, or a famous variety of Kenyan tea, is a recent addition to the variety of teas and is renowned for having the highest level of antioxidants found in a tea. 'We went looking for something else in the jungle and found purple tea leaves growing on a young tea plant. We brought it back, and it showed promising results after being planted on the tea estate, and that's how we got our purple tea. It was auctioned at the Guwahati Tea Auction centre in October 2018 at a striking price of ₹24,501 per kilo,' said Manoj proudly.

Next morning, as my parents and I (they had joined me in Arunachal Pradesh) headed towards Mirrem village, we were joined by Nalanda, the headman of the village. He was a good friend of Parag and was kind enough to come to pick us up. We were soon en route to Mirrem village to experience their centuries-old artisanal tea-crafting methods and to witness the ancient tea trees in the jungle nearby. According to Nalanda, it is from these tea trees that the people of Mirrem pluck tea leaves to make their own tea.

As we reached Mirrem, we were overwhelmed by the welcome we received. Almost the whole village had gathered at Nalanda's place to greet us and had brought their homemade teas as gifts. After introductions, we sat down to lunch in Nalanda's kitchen. While they were serving food, what caught my attention was the squarish wooden platform hanging on top of the earthen stove in the centre of the kitchen, holding many wide trays filled with oxidized tea leaves. 'This is how we dry our tea; it gets naturally dried and develops a beautiful charred, smoky flavour by being kept on top of juihal,' said Nalanda.

After lunch, we gathered in Nalanda's courtyard to watch a demonstration of their ingenious tea-making methods. First, two women washed their feet with herbal soap made from shikakai. Then, they made piles of fresh tea leaves on top of a bamboo mat, stood on top of the piles and started moving their feet in half-circles. They were rolling the tea leaves under their feet to make the juices come out and develop caffeine without damaging the tea leaves. I had seen tea estates using big machines for rolling, and I had also seen tea makers use hand rolling to make their finest teas, but this process of feet rolling was something I had never witnessed or heard of before.

'We pluck our leaves from tea trees in the jungle, so they are broader and more mature as compared to the delicate small ones plucked from tea bushes on estates. Hence, they need a

harder roll and that's why we roll them under our feet,' explained Nalanda. 'But it is not easy to get the perfect roll which yields the desired flavour and colour. So, in order to ensure a balanced roll, we look for a woman of the right weight as someone who is overweight will roll the leaves too hard and an underweight woman won't roll them enough,' he added.

I was still admiring their simple and intelligent approach towards rolling when Oshi, Nalanda's wife, picked up a leaf and pointed to a red vein on the back of the leaf. 'Most of the flavour of the tea comes from this vein, and while plucking, we ensure we select the ones with this red vein.' I had a great urge to see these old tea trees myself and requested them to take me to the jungle.

The next morning, my father and I met Nalanda, Oshi and few other tea artists from the village outside their home, and we trekked along a three-hour trail that led to huge, ancient tea trees. After seeing the neatly arranged, trimmed tea bushes in various tea estates, it was quite a surprise to see Kadu, one of the tea artists in our group, having to climb the tree to pluck the leaves. These trees were at least 25 feet in height and 1.5 feet in width, and they were full of dark green, large, broad leaves with serrated edges. Fifteen minutes after getting to these tea trees, Boke had filled a bamboo mug with tea for me. A light herbal aroma reached my nostrils, and we raised a toast to our wild tea party.

Flavours of Arunachal Pradesh are bold and are best paired with the dishes which mirror equal boldness, and the recipes in this section are my way to do just that.

Chicken Puffs

Leena, Manoj's wife, has the prettiest face and makes the spiciest food. At Donyi Polo, while Manoj takes care of the tea estate, Leena takes care of the guest house. The food I ate at the guest house was made under her supervision, all the recipes belonged to her, and the ingredients were either shopped for or grown by her. One of my favourites on the menu were the momos – silky, translucent pastry draped around spicy-smoky chicken stuffing. As I took one bite, the luscious juices from the stuffing inside dribbled down the corner of my mouth and the steam fogged up my glasses. They were so incredibly delicious that I ate all 10 pieces that I'd been served in one sitting. I then washed it down with some strong tea sweetened with sugar.

It is my dream to one day make silky, paper-thin fresh pastry for momos just like Leena's, but till then, this is my speedy solution to satisfy any cravings of biting into the comforting flavours of chicken encased inside a pastry, especially on a weekday. These puffs are also very handy when you want to show that you have made a massive effort for your guests without having to really do very much.

Prep time: 30 minutes | Baking time: 15–20 minutes | Makes: 8–10

Ingredients

2 tbsp oil
½-inch piece of ginger, chopped
3–4 cloves of garlic, smashed or chopped
2–3 green chillies, finely chopped
Salt, to taste
1 large onion, ground into a paste
1 cup boneless chicken
1 heaped tbsp fresh coriander, chopped

Method

1. Heat the oil in a pan, add the ginger, garlic and green chilli. Sprinkle some salt and sauté for one minute. Add the onion paste and sauté till golden brown. Add the chicken and mix well. Cover and cook on low heat till chicken is done.

2. Now, add the fresh coriander, spring onion, soy sauce and sweet chilli sauce. Mix well. Taste to check for seasoning and adjust accordingly. Cool for at least 30 minutes.

3. Preheat the oven to 180 degrees Celsius for at least 15 minutes. Line a baking tray with baking parchment.

1 spring onion, chopped
1 tsp soy sauce
1tbsp sweet chilli sauce
1 sheet of puff pastry, thawed

4. Roll out the puff pastry and cut it using a medium-sized square or round cookie cutter. Spoon the mixture in one half of the circle/square. Brush the edges with water, fold the other edge to close and press gently to seal. Place in a baking tray and bake for 15–20 minutes or till pastry is puffed and golden.

Ranjeeta Maasi's Hare Matar ki Tikki (Green Pea Cakes)

I think these tikkis were one of the first things to which I contributed my labour as a child. Even then I enjoyed their earthy taste so much that I eagerly participated in shaping them. One of the reasons that these tikkis rank so high in the list of my favourite foods is their light and fresh feel. But the main reason for my undying love for them rests solely upon their charming deliciousness. These are clusters of mushy peas, cumin, green chilli, ginger and lime – heart-warming flavours folded and made into a tikki and seared till crisp – everything that my tea and I love.

Prep time: 30 minutes | Cooking time: 15 minutes | Serves: 3–4

Ingredients

1 tbsp oil + 1 tsp oil
1½ tsp cumin seeds
1 pinch of asafoetida, mixed with 1 tbsp water
1 tsp coriander powder
300 gm fresh peas
1-inch piece of ginger
2 tsp green chillies, finely chopped
Juice of ½ lime
½ tsp black salt
Salt, to taste
2–3 tbsp gram flour

Method

1. Heat the oil in a pan, add the cumin seeds and let them crackle. Add the asafoetida mixed in one tablespoon of water and coriander powder. Sauté for few seconds. Add the peas, grate in ginger, and then add the green chillies, lime juice, black salt and salt. Cover and cook for 4–5 minutes. Transfer to a mixer jar and grind into a smooth paste. Transfer the paste to a bowl.

2. In another pan, dry roast the gram flour for 2–3 minutes. Add to the pea mixture and combine well. Taste and adjust for salt if required.

3. Fill a medium-sized bowl with water and dip your fingers in it. Take a tablespoon of the pea mixture between your palms and shape into a tikki or a cutlet. Make all the tikkis in the same way.

For the chutney (optional)
½ bunch mint leaves
1 bunch coriander leaves
1 clove of garlic
1 green chilli
Juice of ½ lime
2 tbsp curd
1 tsp cumin seeds
Black salt, to taste

4. Heat oil in a shallow pan over medium heat. As soon as it is warm enough, using a flat spatula, gently place the tikkis on the pan and sear till golden brown. Flip them once in between.

5. To make the chutney, add all ingredients to a mixer jar and grind to a smooth paste.

6. Serve with the hot tikkis and strong black Arunachal tea.

Garlic, Chilli and Cheese Toast

Garlic- and chilli-infused cheese melted on top of toasted and buttered bread – need I say anything more?

Prep time: 5 minutes | Cooking time: 10 minutes | Makes: 5

Ingredients

5 tbsp of butter
2 cloves of garlic
2 tsp chilli
5 slices of white bread
10 tbsp of mozzarella cheese

Method

1. Preheat the oven at 200 degrees Celsius.
2. Grease a large roasting tray with some butter.
3. In a medium-sized bowl, add butter, grate in cloves of garlic and add some chilli. Mix properly.
4. Cut the slices of bread diagonally and spread the garlic butter evenly on them. Place them on a roasting tray and sprinkle the mozzarella cheese on top.
5. Put the tray in the oven and bake till the cheese is melted.
6. Switch on the grill and grill it till cheese is slightly caramelized or till it is golden and crispy. Take the tray out and place the slices of bread on a cooling rack. Allow them to cool for 10 minutes before serving.

Allspice Fruit Cake

This is one of those beautiful universal recipes that you first come across during Christmas and is now my favourite choice whenever I am hosting friends who prefer their tea strong because the cake's bold flavours harmonize well with strong tea. With a hint of aromatic spices, texture with a bite to it and punctuated with moistened fruits, this cake is everything I imagine they served in exquisite tea cafés in the UK during the early twentieth century.

I have soaked the fruits in strong tea instead of liquor, but if you wish, replace the tea with same amount of brandy or rum.

Prep time: 30 minutes | Baking time: 150 minutes | Serves: 10–12

Ingredients

225 gm raisins
225 gm dried apricots, chopped
125 gm dried cherries
125 gm dried cherries
125 ml strong tea
225 gm unsalted butter, softened
275 gm brown sugar
5 large eggs
1 tsp orange zest
75 gm almonds, ground
275 gm all-purpose flour
2 tsp allspice powder
1 tsp cinnamon powder

Method

1. Preheat the oven to 150 degrees Celsius. Lightly grease and line a 23-cm cake tin (with 6-cm sides) with baking parchment.

2. Soak the raisins, apricots and dried cherries in strong tea for at least two hours.

3. In a large bowl, beat the butter and sugar till they are creamy. Whisk in the eggs one at a time. Now, add the orange zest, ground almonds and the soaked dried fruit along with the tea in which they were soaking. Sift in the flour, allspice powder and cinnamon powder and fold in gently.

4. Tip the batter into the cake tin and bake for two and a half hours or until a skewer inserted in the centre comes out clean. Let it cool inside the tin for 10 minutes, then unmould it, place it on the cooling rack and let it cool completely.

Double Chocolate Cake

This is the only opportunity to share my favourite chocolate recipe with you as only Arunanchal Pradesh's tea is strong enough not to get intimidated by the bold flavours of chocolate.

The batter will be a bit on the liquidy side, but don't let it bother you, because this is what makes the cake moist and fudgy. Once the cake is baked, it will have a brittle crust on top with a soft squidgy sponge enrobed with melted chocolate sauce underneath. If you are not able to find raspberries in your local store, don't worry, the cake is great just as it is.

Prep time: 30 minutes | Baking time: 40–45 minutes | Serves: 6–8

Ingredients

250 gm salted butter
180 gm sugar
250 gm good-quality dark chocolate
185 gm all-purpose flour
2 tsp baking powder
¼ tsp bicarbonate of soda
40 gm cocoa powder
A pinch of salt
2 large eggs
2 tsp vanilla essence
350 ml lukewarm water

Method

1. Preheat the oven to 180 degrees Celsius. Prepare a 23-cm round cake tin by greasing it with butter and lining the base with baking parchment.

2. Fill a small saucepan with around ½ cup of water and bring it to a simmer over a low flame, but don't allow it to boil.

3. In a medium-sized bowl, add the butter, sugar and chocolate. Place the bowl on top of the saucepan of the simmering water. Allow the chocolate and butter to melt completely, while stirring continuously. Don't let the water touch the bowl, once you feel the water is warm enough, switch off the stove and let the chocolate melt in the steam. This method of melting chocolate in a double boiler is called bain-marie. We are going to use it for the ganache as well.

For the ganache
250 gm good-quality dark chocolate
75 gm butter
100 gm raspberries, for decoration

4. After the chocolate has melted, take the bowl off the saucepan and place it on a cooling rack or on top of a cloth and let it rest as you prepare the other ingredients.

5. In a large mixing bowl, sift in the flour, baking powder, bicarbonate of soda, cocoa powder and salt. Gradually whisk in the melted chocolate. Then, whisk in the eggs, one by one, vanilla essence, and add the lukewarm water a little bit at a time. Once everything is well combined, tip the batter into the baking tin and bake for 40–45 minutes. The skewer test doesn't really work here as cake will be bit moist in the centre.

6. After 45 minutes, take the cake out of the oven and place it on a cooling rack and cool for 30 minutes.

7. Place the chocolate and butter in a bowl and melt in a bain-marie as we did for the cake. Once melted, allow it cool for 15 minutes, then drizzle it all over the chocolate cake and top with some raspberries.

Munnar

The blue sky arched above me as I stood at one of the peaks, seemingly endless tea bushes contoured the hills and beautiful birds dressed in colourful robes and crowns sang in a cheerful, meditative rhythms. It was an oasis of tranquillity.

Munnar is a cosy quaint hill in the state of Kerala. On my tea trail around India, I arrived here a few months after touring the tea estates of Darjeeling, and what I found intriguing here was that unlike Darjeeling, which is divided into 87 separate tea estates, all seven tea gardens in Munnar, encompassing 60 acres of tea plantation, comes under the ownership of Kanan Devan Hills Plantations Company Private Limited (KDHP).

I was staying at a vintage British planter's bungalow-turned-boutique hotel on the highest point of the hill. In the morning, I looked down at tea pastures shimmering with mist. Women pluckers stood facing the sun, their hands joined in the pious position of praying because as Lakshmi, the caretaker of the bungalow and an excellent cook, told me, 'Every morning before starting to pluck the leaves, they pray for a good harvest.' Their prayers couldn't be answered better as KDHP is the only tea estate in India with year-round growth and year-round plucking given their unique two-monsoon climate.

Of these two monsoons, one, famously known as the mango shower, arrives in the month of June, and the other one known as thulam or the north-east monsoon arrives between the months of October and November. Even though the altitude of this hill ranges between 2,000 to 8,000 feet, it still has a tropical climate due to these two seasons of rainfalls it receives. In the world of tea, these climatic conditions means only one thing – no rest either for tea bushes or tea-pluckers.

Only the high range, or the topmost portion of the mountain, has a less humid, wintery climate for most of the year, resulting in lower yields but delicate fruity flavours in the leaves. Leaves from the high range are used to produce specialty teas: orthodox black, white, green and oolong. Apart from the high range, the rest of the garden has the single humid climate, which is suitable for malting and produces leaves with rustic and robust flavours, perfect to be processed into chai patti or CTC. Given the mountainous topography of Munnar, the flavours in its CTC are mellow when compared to Assam's while CTC from plains of Assam is famous for giving the best experience when infused with milk and sugar, Munnar's CTC is good for self-drinking.

I reached Munnar just after summer crowds had cleared and before the damp of rains would set in. The clear view from the peaks revealed how difficult the terrain must have been to conquer back in the nineteenth century.

The story of Munnar becoming a lush, manicured tea estate from a thickly forested, isolated hill, started with Tipu Sultan having to cede this area to the British after the third Anglo-Mysore war in 1792. But the real development began in 1877. After a dispute between the kingdoms of Madras and Travancore drew the East India Company's attention, they deployed John Daniel Munro, who was the superintendent and magistrate of the Cardamom Hills division in Travancore, to settle the issue.

When he got there, Munro could see huge potential in the virgin forests of the Kanan Devan Hills. He leased the land from the Pooniate Raja with the promise to pay annual rent of ₹3000. A few more planters joined Munro including his half-brother A.W. Turner, and together they formed the North Travancore Land Planting and Agricultural Society with a capital of ₹5 lakh. They started by planting tea on 13 acres of land and used the rest of the land for cinchona and coffee. Before the end of the decade, there were 12 resident European planters in the Kanan Devan Hills.

In 1893, Sir John Muir of James Finlay & Co. visited the hills and bought few tea companies. In 1897, James Finlay & Co. formed the KDHP, buying and consolidating all the tea estates in Munnar under a single entity. In 1976, to comply with the Foreign Exchange Regulation Act (FERA) act, they collaborated with Tata Group to form Tata–Finlay Limited, which, in 1983, was fully acquired by the Tatas, giving rise to one of the biggest tea companies in India.

The Tatas ran the company successfully for 18 years, but they started incurring losses from 2001. Their solution to this crisis was very constructive and creative – instead of shutting down operations, they turned to an employee-owned-and-run model. This meant that the management of the whole company, from the plucking to the final packaging of the tea, became the responsibility of employees and, therefore, the profits flowed to them directly as well.

'We saw an immediate growth in profits – having a direct share in the profit made employees much more dedicated towards the company,' said Sanjith. My favourite part of this story was the system of giving out an employee of the year award, and when some years ago, a woman plucker showed promise, she was made the first woman employee to sit on the board. To me, this is more than just a story of profit and loss – it is a story of hopes and dreams and freedom.

One of the most integral parts of KDHP is Shrishti. Its public charitable trust to enable women and the differently abled to be self-sufficient. My experience of Shrishti started in their tea room just below the KDHP headquarters in Munnar. We stopped by the shop for some tea and cake although I had a large traditional Malayali breakfast of puttu and kadala curry (steamed rice cake with black chickpea curry) that morning. But all the adrenaline of new discoveries and fresh air was making me feel hungry and when what's on offer is tea and cake, I really do not need a reason to indulge.

The tea room was very casually styled, and the flavours of cake were seriously delicious. Sanjith told me that all the cakes served there were made at Shrishti. Later, Sanjith took me on a tour of three branches of Shrishti: The Dare School, which was a strawberry preserve-making unit; the deli and confectionary unit, which baked all the moist and tender cakes; and Aranya, the unit for teaching women sustainable farming practices. I was intrigued to meet the bakers, chefs and young interns. The fragrances of cake and bread being baked made me feel strongly connected with them. On my way out, I saw a small, laminated piece of paper on the notice board bearing the words, 'In a free enterprise, the community is not just another stakeholder in the business but is, in fact, the very purpose of its existence – Jamshedji Tata'. And in a true sense, KDHP, in its current avatar, is the manifestation of these golden words of this great visionary.

Soon, the daylight began to dim, we were blessed with a refreshing evening, the sky shining with stars, and I tried to guess the constellations on our back way to our cottages. As we sat down for dinner, the spread was marvellously Malayali: nadan or country-style chicken stew, beetroot thoran, vegetable stew, rice and fried appams. My appetite was greatly whetted by the look of it, and I served myself a generous portion of everything. I took one bite and water started pouring out of my eyes and nose! It was delicious but super spicy. Looking forward to next day, which was reserved for tea tasting, I went to bed, exhausted yet content.

The next day started on a delicious note of another traditional Malayali breakfast – soft, stringy and spongy idiyappams soaked in coconutty egg curry. With the countryside sun and blossoming beauty around me, whole experience felt divine.

I started tasting the various teas with Yezdi Mistry, the tea taster at KDHP, and as he was going down row of cups lined up along the counter, sampling for taste and aroma, he said,

'The art of tea tasting demands a restrained lifestyle.' He explained that further by saying that anything can reduce the sensitivity of the tongue – smoking, alcohol, mouth fresheners or spicy food can have an adverse effect on your tasting abilities and should be avoided.

While telling me more about the KDHP processes, Yezdi said, 'We taste all the batches fired on a day, sometimes more than 10, in order to see what to improve – from the withering to drying. We consider all the required adjustments as per the weather to maintain our grip on quality.' Each sip of Munnar tea carries this passion for perfection of KDHP's employees. Their Orthodox black tea is fruity and delicate with a pronounced note of holy basil (tulsi), a flavour so pious, so fresh, that it can rejuvenate you to your very core, whereas their CTC, although little less intrusive than Assam's, is robust, rich, and full-bodied.

Another charming attraction of the tea tour in Munnar was its tea museum, which showcases the pictures and artifacts revealing the story of how KDHP came into being. The museum is home to original tea rollers used in 1905, the rotor vane, a wheel that was used to generate electricity in the 1920s and a 1913 sundial made by the Art Industrial School at Nazareth in Tamil Nadu. More interestingly, it has a replica of a tea factory which provides an insight into the processing of tea leaves. If you ever want to know exactly how your favourite beverage is made, just visit the Tea Museum at KDHP.

Away from the distractions of modern world, Munnar was a world complete within itself, not smoothly accessible and impossible to leave – god's own country indeed.

Raj Ettan's Sweet Double Roti with Apple Crumble

After completing my tryst with tea in Munnar, I visited Raj Ettan and his wife in Alleppy. I had worked with Raj Ettan on a culinary project for the *Times of Oman* in Muscat before he moved back to his ancestral house in Alleppey and started a bakery with his wife and his brother-in-law. Among all the breads he made me taste during our three-day trip, this was my favourite. To be fair though, it is not exactly a bread, but it lies somewhere between being a cake and a sweet tart. Yeast enlivens the base, whereas the crumble and fruit forms the beautiful crust.

Prep time: 30 minutes | Baking time: 35–40 minutes | Serves: 10

Ingredients

For the double roti or bread

7 gm instant yeast
125 ml lukewarm milk
2 large eggs
1 tsp vanilla extract
350 gm all-purpose flour
50 gm salted butter
50 gm caster sugar

For the topping

½ cup almonds, ground
4 red apples, peeled and roughly chopped
2 tbsp blueberries (optional)
1 tsp cinnamon powder
1 tbsp sugar

Method

1. To make the double roti, in a large bowl or jug, put in the yeast, pour in the lukewarm milk and stir well. Rest for 10 minutes. In the same bowl, add the eggs and vanilla extract. Whisk until everything is combined well. Set aside.

2. In another large bowl, add the flour, butter and sugar. Mix well with your fingertips until you get a breadcrumb-like structure. Gradually add the wet ingredients to the dry ingredients and knead a dough. Let the dough rest for at least 1 hour.

3. Preheat the oven to 180 degrees Celsius. Grease and line a large, rectangular baking tray (9x13 inches) with baking parchment, leaving a bit hanging out of one corner. This makes it easy to unmould the bread.

For the crumble
75 gm all-purpose flour
50 gm caster sugar
100 gm cold butter
½ tsp nutmeg, grated

4. Prepare the crumble by putting the flour, sugar, butter and nutmeg in a bowl and mixing them with your fingertips till they resemble breadcrumbs.Place it in the refrigerator.

5. To continue making the double roti, sprinkle the working surface with some flour, place the risen dough, punch it to get the air out. Use a rolling pin to roll out the dough to a size that will fit into the baking tray. Carefully transfer to the tray and sprinkle the almonds, chopped apples, blueberries, cinnamon and sugar across the dough. Finally, top with the crumble. Bake for 35–40 minutes.

6. Remove from the oven, cool for 10–15 minutes and cut.

Cinnamon Buns

While I was in Munnar, shopping for spices and teas was inevitable. Having bought some cinnamon, all I could think of was being in my kitchen and baking a fresh batch of cinnamon buns. Nothing beats the heartwarming aroma of cinnamon buns wafting from the oven, especially during Christmas. But why should you wait for Christmas to enjoy a cinnamon bun, when you can bake them any other day of the year or when your mood calls for their cosy comfort? These cinnamon buns taste delicious and are so easy to make that the thought of buying the ones available in the supermarket will never cross your mind. Their cinnamon-laced warmth and subtle sweetness is meant to be enjoyed with a cup of strong black tea from Munnar. Pay close attention to the measurements mentioned in the recipe – they are crucial if you want to get a crisp swirl in your buns.

Prep time: 10 minutes | Cooking time: 15–20 minutes | Makes: 15–20

Ingredients

200 gm full fat milk
200 gm butter
2 medium eggs
½ tsp of vanilla essence
600 gm all-purpose flour
50 gm caster sugar
A pinch of salt
7 gm or 1 sachet of dry yeast or
25 gm fresh yeast
24-piece cupcake tin

For the filling

125 gm unsalted butter
150 gm soft brown sugar
2 tsp of cinnamon

Method

1. Add the milk and butter to a saucepan and place it on stove. Let it heat gently till the butter is melted. Then turn off the heat and place it aside. After it is cooled, whisk in the eggs and vanilla essence.

2. In a large bowl, add flour, sugar, pinch of salt and yeast. Use a spatula to gently mix everything together.

3. Now, gradually stir in the liquid ingredients into the flour mixture while stirring to form a loose dough. Turn the dough on the kneading surface and knead it by pushing gently with your palm till it is smooth.

4. Place the dough in an oiled bowl, cover it with a tea towel or a cling film. Place the bowl in a warm area and allow it to prove for 45 minutes.

For the glaze
1 egg
2 tbsp of milk

5. While the dough is proofing, prepare the filling. Mix the butter, brown sugar and cinnamon in a bowl and set it aside.

6. After the dough is proofed, turn it out on a lightly floured kneading surface. Use a rolling pin to roll the dough into a rectangle of at least 50 x 25 cm.

7. Spread the filling evenly on the dough and roll it length wise into a cylindrical shape. Slice it into pieces measuring 2.5–3 cm. You will get approximately 16 to 17 pieces.

8. Slightly butter the cupcake tin. Place each slice into a cupcake hole in the tin. Allow it to prove for 20 more minutes.

9. Meanwhile, preheat the oven at 220 degrees Celsius for 20 minutes.

10. Mix the egg and milk in a small bowl to prepare the glaze. Whisk them together. Very gently, apply the glaze to the top of the buns once they are proved. Place the tray inside the oven for 20 minutes.

11. Once they are golden brown on top, bring the tray out and allow it to cool for 5 minutes. Remove the cinnamon buns from the tray and place them on a cooling rack. Allow them to cool for 15 minutes before serving.

Breakfast Bars

These bars are a lifesaver on the days I have no time to eat breakfast, or no time to get a bite in between meetings. On those days, I wake up in the morning, get ready, grab these bars, fill my tumbler with tea and get on with my day.

Prep time: 10 minutes | Cooking time: 15–20 minutes | Makes: 15 bars approx.

Ingredients

200 gm white and red quinoa
Sesame seeds
Peanuts
100 gm rolled oats
300 gm maple syrup
150 gm almond butter
25 gm coconut oil
A pinch of salt
50 gm raisins
50 gm flaked almonds
1 tbsp sunflower seeds
1 tbsp pumpkin seeds
1 tbsp chia seeds
1 tsp vanilla extract

Method

1. Preheat the oven to 180 degrees Celsius. Line a sheet pan or a cookie baking tray with baking parchment.

2. Heat a pan over medium heat and add quinoa and peanut. Dry roast them till they start to turn golden. Transfer to a bowl and set aside. In the same pan, dry roast the oats till they start to change colour. Transfer to the same bowl.

3. In a saucepan, put in the maple syrup, almond butter, coconut oil and salt. Melt over a medium-low heat until smooth.

4. Add raisins, flaked almonds, sunflower seeds, pumpkin seeds, chia seeds and vanilla extract to the bowl with quinoa and oats.

5. Pour the melted liquid ingredients over the dry ingredients. Mix well and then empty the mixture into the sheet pan or cookie baking tray. Use a spatula to even out the mixture in the shape of a 10x5-inch rectangle. Place the tray inside the oven and bake for 15 to 20 minutes or until golden on top.

6. Remove the tray from the oven and place it on a cooling rack. Allow it to cool for a minimum of one hour, then place the slab on the chopping board and chop it into around 15 bars.

Fig and Coconut Energy Moments

These nutty, caramelly, fruity clusters of energy are lifesavers on the days when I have no time to sit down to eat.

You can use dates in place of figs as they both add the same kind of caramelly sweetness. Goji berries add a fruity tang, and I recommend not replacing them, but in case you are not able to find them, try dried cranberries.

Prep time: 10 minutes | Cooking time: None! | Makes: 20 approx.

Ingredients

130 gm dried figs
130 gm cashew nuts
60 gm goji berries
2 tbsp chia seeds
100 gm + 2 tbsp desiccated coconut

Method

1. Spread the desiccated coconut on a plate.

2. Add all the other ingredients, apart from the 2 tablespoons of desiccated coconut, to a blender or to a food processor and blend into as smooth a mixture as possible.

3. Take about 1 tablespoon of the mixture in between your palms and roll it into a ball. Place it on top of the desiccated coconut on the plate. Roll it around till the ball gets a good coating of coconut. Repeat the same with the rest of the mixture.

Keema Pav

The secret to a delectable keema filling for pav lies in the generous use of fat and zero use of water. I would suggest not taking the low-fat route for this recipe. It's a special dish usually eaten on a special occasion, and every special occasion needs to be celebrated with plentiful of luxurious flavours.

Prep time: 10 minutes | Cooking time: 45 minutes | Makes: 5–6

Ingredients

2 tbsp of ghee
2 tbsp of oil
½-inch piece of cinnamon
2 pods of green cardamom
1 big black cardamom
5–6 black pepper corns
1 bay leaf
2 large onions, chopped
A pinch of salt
1 tbsp ginger, chopped
1 tbsp garlic, chopped
1 tsp turmeric powder
1 tbsp red chilli powder
1 tbsp coriander powder
1 tsp garam masala powder
¼ cup of yogurt
500 gm minced lamb (keema)
Juice of 1 lime
Chopped coriander, to serve
Pav, to serve
2–3 whole green chillis, to serve

Method

1. Heat ghee and oil in a wok, and add cinnamon, green and black cardamom, pepper corns and bay leaf. Sauté for 30 seconds. Now add chopped onion, stir in a pinch of salt and sauté on low flame till golden brown.

2. Now add ginger, garlic and turmeric powder, red chilli powder, coriander powder, garam masala powder and mix well. Sauté for 1 minute.

3. Stir in the yogurt and allow it to simmer for 4–5 minutes.

4. Add minced lamb, salt and mix thoroughly. Cover and cook on low flame for 30 minutes.

5. Stir in lime juice and chopped coriander. Reserve some coriander to sprinkle on top after serving.

6. Serve it on a platter, with some butter toasted pav and some onions, green chillis and lemon.

Falafel

I love falafels because of the burst of flavours I get in a single bite – the crispy crust on the outside with a soft gooey centre. For me, everything in it, from the complex textures to the earthy freshness, calls out for a cup of strong black tea afterwards.

A plate of falafels reflects the plentifulness of traditional platters, especially when served with a tahini dip, some salad and a stack of pita bread. You can either dip the falafel in the tahini dip and have it with the salad and just pop it in your mouth, or make your own falafel wrap by applying the tahini dressing on the pita bread and topping it off with the falafel and salad.

Prep time: 15 minutes | Cooking time: 15–20 minutes | Makes: 5–6

Ingredients

For falafels

250 gm soaked chickpeas
1 big onion, quartered
2 big cloves of garlic
1 bunch of coriander
½ bunch of parsley
1 tsp of cumin powder
1 tsp of red chilli powder
½ tsp black salt
2 tbsp sesame seeds
Salt, to taste
1 tbsp baking powder
Oil, to fry

Method

1. Add chickpeas, onion, garlic, coriander, parsley, cumin powder, red chilli powder, black salt, sesame seeds, salt and baking powder in a blender and blend into a coarse paste.

2. Take the mixture out on a plate and roll medium-sized balls out of it.

3. Heat oil to medium degree, add the falafels, and fry on medium flame till brownish, flip in between. Take it out on a plate lined with tissue paper. Keep it aside.

4. In a bowl, add tahini, yogurt, garlic, lime and salt to prepare the tahini dip and whisk till everything is well combined.

For the tahini dip
4 tbsp tahini
5–6 tbsp yogurt
1 clove of garlic, grated
Juice of 1 lime
Salt, to taste

For the salad
1 cucumber, minced
1 tomato, minced
1 onion, minced
½ bunch of parsley, minced
Juice of ½ lemon
Salt, to taste
Pita bread, to serve

5. In a separate bowl, add cucumber, tomato, onion, parsley, lime juice and salt and mix well.

6. Arrange the falafels, the dip and the salad on a platter, any way you prefer and enjoy with tea.